Ultrasounds

Basque Literature Series

No. 9

Ultrasounds

Basque Women Writers on Motherhood

Selected and Edited by Gema Lasarte

Translated by Nere Lete

"A Draft" by Ixiar Rozas translated by
Linda White and Elizabeth Macklin

Series Editor
Mari Jose Olaziregi

Center for Basque Studies
University of Nevada, Reno

This book was published with generous financial support from the Basque Government.

Center for Basque Studies

Basque Literature Series, No. 9
Basque Literature Series Editor: Mari Jose Olaziregi

Center for Basque Studies
University of Nevada, Reno
Reno, Nevada 89557
http://basque.unr.edu

Book design: Kimberly Daggett
Cover design: Daniel Montero

Original publication information following text in
Acknowledgments

Library of Congress Control Number: 2014956284

Contents

INTRODUCTION

Gema Lasarte

Motherhood is a key theme in contemporary feminist criticism, and, in particular, the difficulties that motherhood poses for writers. Thus, a statement such as that by Ellen Moers has become widely known: excellence in motherhood is directly connected to diminished creativity.[1] Virginia Wolf considered it extremely difficult to have children and be a writer at the same time.[2] Among Basque writers, Lourdes Oñaederra explains that she has renounced motherhood in order to have the freedom to pursue her profession.[3] Laura Mintegi and Arantxa Urretabizkaia Bejarano said that they had children late in life because they gave priority to their writing. Geraldine Nichols, considering works written by women in Spain between 1990 and 2001, has analyzed those writers that leaned either in favor of or against motherhood.[4] Gema Lasarte completed similar research in her doctoral thesis in which she studied motherhood in contemporary Basque fiction between 1979 and 2009.[5]

---

1. Biruté, *La novela femenina contemporánea*, 16.
2. This idea is developed in her essay *A Room of One's Own*.
3. Urkiza, *Zortzi unibertso, zortzi idazle*, 272.
4. Redondo Goicoechea, *Jóvenes narradoras de los noventa*, 192–207.
5. Lasarte, *Pertsonaia protagonista femeninoen ezaugarriak eta bilakaera euskal narratiba garaikidean.*

Through the years, many authors in the field of feminist criticism have completed and published diverse and well-developed research regarding motherhood. But the work of three theorists in particular has established the main lines of study: Simone de Beauvoir's *Le Deuxième Sexe* (1949), Shulamith Firestone's *The Dialect of Sex* (1971), and Adrienne Rich's *Of Woman Born: Motherhood as Experience and Institution* (1976). More contemporary research has continued to delve into the problems of modern motherhood. Let's examine, if briefly, what has been said in these works and about them. At first glance, Simone de Beauvoir's analysis might seem to exclusively expose the negative aspects of motherhood. However, Linda Zirelli argues that exposing the challenges and the negative aspects of motherhood is nothing but a discursive strategy. As part of that strategy, Beauvoir criticized a motherhood imposed upon women. Zirelli states that for male authority figures of the time, like priests, philosophers, and men of science motherhood-happiness was restricted to the mother-fetus paradigm. For Beauvoir that very same concept provoked struggle and difference of opinion. In Zirelli's view, Beauvoir was making a gesture toward a new interpretation of motherhood.[6] However, it must be said that both equality feminism and materialist feminism have dealt with motherhood under the realm of egalitarianism. This means that motherhood has brought with it challenges for women stepping into the professional, political, and cultural spheres as it has been considered an exclusionary role. Shulamith Firestone (1971) agrees with this perspective and states that women have been oppressed because of their biological function. In short, women's oppression began with reproduction and has followed in a continuum. Lastly,

---

6. Zerilli, "A Process without a Subject."

Adrienne Rich proposes two interpretations of motherhood; motherhood as institution and motherhood as pleasure, knowledge and empowerment. Rich states that motherhood, perceived as institution, confuses instinct with intelligence, self-advancement with generosity and attention toward others with attention to the self. Therefore, Rich (1976) comes to the conclusion that certain matters which threaten the institution of motherhood like abortion, lesbianism, or motherhood outside of a heterosexual relationship, are considered dangerous. Many of the "motherhoods" that we will offer in this anthology will be samples of such deviation.

Biruté Ciplijauskait (1994) wrote that most literary works portray motherhood in two ways. On one hand, it is a destructive force, ruining independence and self-advancement and, on the other hand, a continuation of a mythical power. Within this power, the function of the body and the dialectics of the spoken are proposed. These readings will make apparent many of the negative aspects outlined by Firestone and equality feminism and, on the other hand, will present motherhood as the source of one's experiences and the builder of identity. As Teresa del Valle states, motherhood is constructed from the knowledge of one's own body on which many women base their identity and memory.[7]

Through the stories in this anthology, we explore motherhood, and we can confirm what Lucienne Goldmann stated, that there are analogies between literary structures and social structures.[8] The mother protagonists in the selection we present have built their personal histories on motherhood. We come to ratify what Basque feminist anthropologists, Carmen Diéz and Eli Imaz have separately noted, that

---

7. Del Valle, "Identidad, memoria y juegos de poder," 21.
8. Goldamann. *Pour une sociologie du roman.*

the Basque family and motherhood are changing, and that mothers are the catalysts of such change.[9] In Imaz's words, the changing motherhood and family must be ranked as one of the most important transformations taking place among gender relations. Women are changing and along with them the family and relationships between the couple. "Maternity is perceived as a main scenario, if not the most important, in the redefinition of gender relations."[10] For Imaz, the main consequences of this shift are: an increase of different types of families, the appearance of new types of motherhood, and different ways of being a mother.

Imaz lists the following as some examples of new types of motherhood: working mothers, older mothers, mothers outside of marriage, lesbian mothers, and single mothers. We have found these types of motherhoods in the Basque short story oeuvre and we will unveil them in the following pages.

Before reaching these conclusions however, it should be noted that the representations of motherhood have been created through visual and discursive symbolic constructions. These representations are the composition of a set of ideas, beliefs, and meanings. They explain the world and we can find their most meaningful examples in stereotypes, body metaphors, and norms. Besides assisting us in envisioning motherhood, norms adopt a great importance because they dictate our attitude. Therefore, this anthology of motherhood offers an ultrasound of the construction of symbolic motherhood.

To conclude this discussion of motherhood, we must mention two categories: The traditional *hegemonic motherhood*, which emphasizes norms, roles, stereotypes, and pres-

---

9. Díez, "¿Maternidad: hecho natural?" and "Maternidad y orden social"; Imaz, *Mujeres gestantes, madres en gestación.*
10. Imaz, *Mujeres gestantes, madres en gestación,* 10.

ents very specific body metaphors. In this case, motherhood is understood as a natural act, something private, biological and, at most, psychological, something far from science and hardly an object of study. Any scientific consideration has been limited to the medical field of obstetrics and gynecology, and thus, relegated to the patriarchal discourse of motherhood.

However, the *emerging models* of motherhood (as is evident in the work coordinated by Del Valle[11]) have their own identity and, while not outside of the normative model, have acquired new meaning and importance. They convey new relationships. Undoubtedly, most of the motherhood profiles in this anthology are representations of emerging motherhoods. They display a consciousness, a clear intention for change. Therefore, besides symbolic constructions, we can speak of a strategy of quest and change, in short, a process of agency.[12]

If these are contemporary representations of motherhood, the question that follows is: What is motherhood? What are the main axes that shape motherhood? Is it the creation, the development, the reproduction, the identity, the social position, the social role? Thus far, in hegemonic motherhood, there has been a systematic omission of these axes. On the contrary, in emerging motherhood, new values are surfacing, and these are evident throughout most of the stories selected for this anthology.

While the unifying criterion for this collection, short stories written between 1983 and 2013, is the theme of motherhood, we have also taken other issues into account.

---

11. Del Valle, *Modelos emergentes en los sistemas y las relaciones de género*.
12. This concept claims subjectivity, to function as a subject; to understand the role of protagonist as a position.

In this anthology women writers are the protagonists, more accurately; the center of this work is modern storytelling authored by women over the past three decades. Contemporary short story writing is the most recent modern genre to surface in Basque literature, beginning with Anjel Lertxundi's *Hunik arrats artean* (Wait until dusk, 1970). Nevertheless, two short decades have been enough to establish the genre. In the 1980s there was a great expansion of this genre and Arantxa Urretabizkaia Bejarano's first collection of short stories was published during this time. In 1990, Jasone Osoro Igartua and Arantxa Iturbe burst onto the scene. But the most important contribution of women to the genre came in the twenty-first century with Eider Rodriguez, Uxue Apaolaza Larrea, Katixa Agirre Miguélez, Karmele Jaio Eiguren, Uxue Alberdi Estibaritz, and Ana Urkiza. This new context has provided women writers the opportunity to be heard and, as examples of their work, we have two short story collections, *Gutiziak* (Cravings, 2000) and *Orgasmus* (2010).

The third criterion is based on the intrinsic aesthetic and literary value of the stories. We tried to offer stories that are about fifteen pages long, but have occasionally transgressed that limit since some stories are very short, micro stories that read as capsules: the stories of Uxue Apaolaza Larrea, Ana Urkiza, Arantxa Urretabizkaia Bejarano, and Aurelia Arkotxa, for example. Others are longer narratives structured more like novels, which, after the 1970s, have been referred to as "short story cycles."[13] Regarding the aesthetic value of the stories, we must point out the new perspectives created by blending different styles and tones. These perspectives are

---

13. Olaziregi, *Intimismoaz haraindi,* 48. There is a connection between all these stories: either through themes, the types of narrators, characters and places.

particularly evident in the writing of Karmele Jaio Eiguren, Uxue Alberdi Estibaritz, Katixa Agirre Miguélez, Uxue Apaolaza Larrea, Eider Rodriguez, and Ixiar Rozas.

There are also important examples of genre hybridization in this anthology, such as the blending of prose and poetry of Miren Agur Meabe, Aurelia Arkotxa, and Irati Jimenez Uriarte: the blending of the written and spoken word, what is sung and told. Summarizing, this anthology proposes a new worldview through intimate gazes, advances women as protagonists, reflects on motherhood as a fundamental keystone, and offers a diverse array of styles and tones.

Let's consider, if briefly, each author's individual work compiled in this anthology. From Aurelia Arkotxa's book *Fragmentuak* (2006) we have selected the stories titled "Cordelia," "Word Stalactites" ("Hitz-estalaktitak"), "Kaki Tree" ("Kaki ondoa"), "Stabat mater," and "By Car" ("Berebilez"). The anthology opens with these pieces because of the wide spectrum of motherhood types presented in them: Mothers as transmitters of language and culture, as trees embodying the *axis-mundi*, mothers throughout history. In order to carve word memories Arkotxa loves writing short pieces or *fragments*, "sparks, condensed tales," which is exactly what her book consists of.[14] She acknowledges that when she writes, she uses familiar landscapes, people, animals, plants, books, and events, but admits that writing is a difficult task: "for me 'description,' for example, to paint a tree using words, is the most difficult and beautiful type of writing."[15] She loves crossbreeding genres and mentions Pascal Quignarden's work as an example, wondering if his pieces should be considered novels, essays, or poetry. In her opinion they

---

14. Urkiza, *Zortzi unibertso, zortzi idazle*, 123.
15. Ibid., 147.

are a combination of the three. In her work *Septentrio* (2001), she fuses poetry and narration while in *Fragmentuak*, she goes further, pushing the hybridization of genres to its limit. Aurelia Arkotxa erases the borders between journalism and literature and, with fellow travelers Li Po, Emily Dickinson, and Ovidio, she proposes new geographies for Basque literature. We start the journey of this anthology through them.

We have selected Uxue Apaolaza Larrea's "Shopping Cart" ("Karrotxoa") and "Familian" ("In the Family") from her collection *Umeek gezurra esaten dutenetik* (From the time children told lies, 2005). If we were to highlight the innovative contribution of her collection to Basque literature, we would undoubtedly emphasize the rawness her stories emanate. She writes about uncomfortable themes like suicide, drugs, loneliness, abortion, and casual sex, bringing readers to a moral chill[16] and adding a notch to Raymond Carver's dirty realism. Besides the raw tone of her stories Apaolaza Larrea's book introduces something else: the deconstruction of gender. The desire to deconstruct stereotypes and gender roles is evident in the stories we have selected. A raw point of view and dry tone accompanied by measured words in an increasingly tense narrative tone culminate at the final blow where the reader may look at motherhood through another prism: the unexpected.

In an effort to continue defining motherhood, we have selected Maite Gonzalez Esnal's story "He Wanted to Clip Her Wings" ("Hegoak ebaki nahi zizkion") from the collection *Gutiziak* (Cravings, 2000). Maite Gonzalez explains the meaning of the word *gutizia* in connection with the deeply rooted idea of motherhood in Basque culture. This sto-

---

16. Gorka Bereziartua, "Gure belaunaldi zikin hau (erabili dezakegu hitz hau eguneko ordu hauetan?)." EremuLauak.com, January 6, 2006.

ry talks about the experience of the author herself and puts forth what motherhood is from the father figure's perspective. That is the reason Maite Gonzalez has played with the title of the well-known and acclaimed song by Mikel Laboa. For the father, cravings are the reason to satisfy the mother. For the mother, on the contrary, they are just another way to have her wings clipped. Born in 1943, Maite Gonzalez worked mostly writing and disseminating children's literature. Her story is of significant value as it invites the reader to see and read through a light veil, the importance that gastronomy and culture have had upon the hegemonic concept of motherhood.

We selected the story "Seed" ("Hazia") from Eider Rodriguez's *Katu jendea* (Cat people, 2010). We wholeheartedly agree with Jon Kortazar when he states that Eider Rodriguez brings prominence to silence. Her writing is minimalist. All that the characters have is a name and, stylistically, through a process of elimination, all that remains is bare emotion. The reader's task is to fill in the blanks to understand the tragic bitterness of the stories.[17] This is precisely what happens in "Seed". The main character ponders motherhood and shares her tragic and cynical point of view. She is alone at home with her baby, thinking of what she has given up and how people view her differently. Through a lyric-ironic and melancholy tone, she offers a limited vision of motherhood through a lense of realism. Eider Rodriguez's writing has the unique ability to transform each story into an image: a mother looking out her home window, a cigarette in her mouth, and a newborn nearby. Indescribable. A performance. Irony.

We have also selected Miren Agur Meabe's *Zazpi orduak*

---

17. Jon Kortazar, "Haragiaren komunikazioa," *El País*, February 25, 2008.

(Seven hours, 2010). Throughout her trajectory as a writer she has blurred the line between literary genres. Sometimes she has written poetry, other times she has focused on novels, specifically children's and young adult novels. These two short stories, whose protagonist is Doltza, are two such examples since they are stories for young and adult readers alike. These are lyric and symbolic narrations in which the importance of the word is acclaimed and connected to motherhood as can also be seen in Arkotxa's "Word Stalactites" and "By Car." Through a prose bordering on poetry, Meabe offers readers a glimpse of fantastic literature. In order to capture the sensibility of childhood, she transports the reader to a mythical world and takes advantage of poetic prose and verse common in oral traditions, making her stories ones that can be either read or told.

Ana Urkiza's short stories are part of the *Bekatuak* collection (Sins, 2005). The large dose of humor that Urkiza brings to this little catalog of sins, the seriousness of the topic, and the stories' ironic tone make the book very appealing. Urkiza's short story collection is written in a style reminiscent of the minimalist Katherine Mansfield. Carefully measured words describe everyday life. She plays with micro stories such as in her works *Desira izoztuak* (Frozen desires, 2001) or her book of aphorisms, *Atzorako geratu dena* (What is left for yesterday, 2011). *Bekatuak* is a polyphonic book as the voices change constantly. The narrator uses the first, third, and second person. Additionally the time of the narration switches and we can find the same passage told from different perspectives. We have selected three of Urkiza's stories in which motherhood is explored. "Faraway Ties" ("Urrutiko Lokarriak"), Making a Boy ("Mutila egiten"), "A New Cinderella" ("Errauskiñe berria"). She presents some of the negative aspects of motherhood mentioned by Shulamith Firestone, such as undesired pregnancies. The protagonists are presented as agents who are managing motherhood as subject. We will leave aside the norms and traditions of hegemonic motherhood and will begin reading new paradigms of motherhood.

We have selected two short stories, "I Bet She Has Curly Hair!" ("Baietz ile kizkurra izan") and "Two Pimples" ("Bi grano") from Arantxa Iturbe's *Lehenago zen berandu* (It had been late earlier, 1997) and *Gutiziak* short story collections. Iturbe presents the everyday lives of two young women in their own words. Both protagonists get pregnant and both stories ironically wink at romantic love, reminding us of Milan Kundera's humorous love stories. But in Iturbe's case, she presents active women and speaks of emerging motherhoods, of agencies, and the rights that women have to make decisions related to their bodies and pregnancies. Iturbe's stories are short, humorous, and rhythmically lively. Her writing style is constructed upon a dialectic with reality, with strokes of orality and freshness which she obtains through a direct style, brisk rhythm, measured words, and an avoidance of superfluous elements.[18] The ironic and humorous endings of these short stories are worth emphasizing because of their humor and punch.

This anthology continues introducing new mothers through Jasone Osoro Igartua's "Love Is a Puzzle " ("Maitasuna puzzle bat da") *Korapiloak* (Knots, 2001) that looks at working mothers, older mothers, and those who have become mothers outside of the institution of marriage. The included story grapples with the themes of abandonment and

---

18. Gutierrez Retolaza, *90eko hamarkadako narratiba berria: Literatur kritika*, 114.

the Oedipal syndrome through a protagonist who is a single mother that has abandoned her son. Like her first book, *Tentazioak* (Temptations, 1998), *Korapiloak* is a short story collection that is easy to read and displays a carefully designed rhythm and structure. "Love Is a Puzzle" is a lively story that develops through the conversations between mother and son in their first encounter. The collection is full of descriptions and stories that might appear the eccentric through their description of body parts and the obscene by describing secretions. The stories have the ability to move between daily burdens and the absurd through what at times could be considered grotesque stories but which are taken to a realistic and indefinite time.[19]

Garazi Kamio Anduaga's "Panenka" has been selected from her collection *Beste norbaiten zapatak* (Someone else's shoes, 2012). Kamio Anduaga's strong use of imagery is worth mentioning. It also has an interesting analysis that the main character, a mother, makes about motherhood. She reflects about the mother-grandmother-daughter relationship. As a daughter, she explains how motherhood is changing: as a daughter she speaks from the loser's perspective, and now that she is a mother and thought things had changed, she realizes that she remains in the same position. The mother and protagonist of the story explains how new types of motherhood are emerging yet they continue to strongly mimic the traditional forms.

The next story included is Ixiar Rozas's "A Draft" ("Korronteak") from *Mende berrirako ipuinak* (Stories for the new century) from the anthology version (2005). The Basque publisher Erein published this work in 2001 as *Sartu, kor-*

---

19. Ana Urkiza, "Maitasuna puzzle bat da," *Euskaldunon Egunkaria*, April 28, 2001.

rontea dabil (Come in, it is drafty). It was the first story in the book and received the Donostia Hiria award. The focus of the entire anthology is on the affective relationship between the characters and their loneliness. The inclusion of one of Edward Hopper's posters in the original text not only speaks of loneliness but paints it. The plot is simple and the characters are ordinary people. They are headed to Paris in search of something, as Rojo might say, to the city, to the site of the world's metonymy, by train.[20] The story takes place in the train where they meet, in the course of everyday life. Rozas loves ellipsis and the camera and, through a glance that is suggestive more than direct, she looks outward like a woman in one of Hopper's paintings, sitting on a bed, her gaze directed toward a window. Meanwhile, the son is headed to Paris looking for his father, fulfilling his mother's deathbed request.

Arantxa Urretabizkaia Bejarano's "Because I Am Expecting You" ("Espero zaitudalako") was published as part of her collection *Aspaldian espero zaitudalako ez nago sekula bakarrik*, (I am never alone because I am expecting you, 1983) Mari Jose Olaziregi argues that this collection must be placed within Basque literature's short story boom of the 1980s. At that time, when North America's dirty realism and South America's magical realism were influencing Basque literature's short story tradition, Urretabizkaia Bejarano did something different: inner storytelling. Olaziregi recognizes forbidden love in this story that narrates the unspeakable love that Coro, the nun, feels for the baby Jesus over four days every holiday season.[21] Is this story about forbidden love and unrealized motherhood or does it show a deconstructed view

---

20. Rojo, *Egungo euskal ipuingintzaren historia*, 282.
21. Olarziregi, *Intimismoaz haraindi*, 48.

of the Virgin Mother who became pregnant without having a sexual relationship? This story's title infers pregnancy, waiting, awaiting, expectancy, and is the only one in this anthology that provides a mystic reading of motherhood.

Begoña Bilbao Alboniga's "Spilled Water Cannot Be Re-Gathered" ("Isuritako ura ez da batzen"); *Ipuin Izugarriak*, (Amazing stories, 2004) shows a more terrible side of motherhood. We should consider this story, which received the Irun Saria award in 1999 within the category of dark ruralism. This story takes place before the first half of last century and establishes the chronotope around life in Basque rural society and underscores the ideological burden that motherhood carried for women at that time. Like her story, Bilbao Alboniga's literary career was also wonderful and astonishing. She completed her Basque philology degree in 1983 at the University of Deusto when she was fifty-five years old. It is then when she began publishing and receiving awards for her short stories and her novel. She wrote until her death in 2005.

In order to complete the motherhood paradigms and paradoxes of motherhood, we have selected Irati Elorrieta's "Torn Landscapes" ("Paisaia urratuak") from her work *Orgasmus*. This is an extremely interesting story not only because it is about new types of motherhood but also because it talks about new types of happiness. The story is written from two different perspectives, that of the father and of the mother. The couple has separated and they have two daughters together. This tension is the origin of the mismatched and torn landscapes. This story, which is the longest in the anthology, dissolves the boundary between a short story and a novel. Additionally, it introduces broken, main characters who depart from their feelings and thoughts. This story is connected to the novel *Burbuilak*, (Bubbles) written by Elorrieta in 2008. As its editor, Inazio Mujika stated, Elorrieta's work was a novel made up of short stories. Those stories were narrative and lyrical texts that also emanated motherhood following a paused, undetermined style swollen by pregnancy.

We have attempted to contrast the definition of motherhood between hegemonic and emergent motherhoods by examining the interpretations that people make of motherhood. In the following stories the focus shifts to the unborn. On one hand, Uxue Alberdi Estibaritz's "Gifts" ("Opariak"), and on the other hand, Karmele Jaio Eiguren's "Ultrasounds" ("Ekografiak") from her collection titled *Ez naiz ni*, (It is not me, 2012). They are consecutive so that the reader notices how differently the stories of both pregnancies have been constructed. "Gifts" talks about a baby who has not yet been born, about the desire to shape the personality of one who is yet to be born. "Ultrasounds," on the contrary, is a story about the loneliness of a mother who has decided to adopt a baby alone. However, both stories are about issues raised around motherhood and, consequently, about the influence exercised on motherhood. Uxue Alberdi Estibaritz and Karmele Jaio Eiguren are both important figures with very different styles. Alberdi Estibaritz's tone is sharp and cold while Jaio Eiguren's is tender and close. Both stories show a critical interpretation of the traditional family model and highlight the thoughts of the characters who are about to become mothers without a heterosexual partner.

During the last decades, feminist anthropology speaks of new family paradigms and different ways to experience motherhood. We close this anthology with two stories that depict other types of motherhood. Irati Jimenez Uriarte's "The Tears of the Orange Peel" ("Laranja azalaren negarra"). Jimenez Uriarte wrote this story before she published her acclaimed novel, *Nora ez dakizun hori* (You who have lost your way, 2009). They present commonalities. Both have been constructed closely following audio-visual scripts and in both the grandmothers adopt the role of the protagonists' mothers. As Iñaki Aldekoa states on the book's jacket, this story narrates a personal journey, a journey of the protagonist toward adulthood. Every step of the way, grandmother stays beside her. The child has grown up with the grandmother and when her grandmother dies the child also symbolically dies, allowing the adult to be born. All the while, the mother is present but appears as a mere anecdote. Poetry and narrative intertwine to express the feelings of the protagonist. Time is realist and infinite and the space is the mother's house and bakery. Though the story has lyric touches, apart from the title, the story is very realistic. It speaks of loneliness, incomprehension, and obesity.

To conclude this anthology, we have selected Katixa Agirre Miguélez's "Guy Fawkes's Treason" ("Guy Fawkesen traizioa") *Habitat* (2009) a story that invites us to consider motherhood from yet another perspective. We have opened with Arkotxa's lyricisms, a polyhedral gaze at motherhood, followed by raw, humorous, sharp, melancholic, cold, and tender tones. To wrap up the anthology, we have selected a great storyteller: Katixa Agirre Miguélez, who is well known for her humorous and ironic tone. The story revolves around the days the protagonist must spend as a mother to her boyfriend's son. The well-developed story bursts with irony and humor, without superfluous words and with an ending designed to make the reader stop in their tracks. "Trapped. With no escape. We are not sure why."

Bibliography

Ciplijauskaité, Biruté. *La novela femenina contemporánea (1970–1985): Hacia una tipología de la narración en primera persona*. Barcelona: Anthoropos, 1994.

Del Valle, Teresa. "Identidad, memoria y juegos de poder." *Dena, Revista Cultural* 2 (1994): 14–21.

Del Valle, Teresa. *Modelos emergentes en los sistemas y las relaciones de género*. Madrid: Narcea, 2002.

Díez, Carmen. "¿Maternidad: hecho natural? / ¿constructo ideológico?" *Bitarte* 7 (1995): 81–93.

———. "Maternidad y orden social: Vivencias de cambio." In *Perspectivas feministas desde la antropología social*, edited by Teresa del Valle, 155–85. Barcelona: Ariel, 2000.

Goldamann, Lucien. *Pour une sociologie du roman*. Paris: Gallimard, 1964.

Gutierrez Retolaza, Iratxe. *90eko hamarkadako narratiba berria: Literatur kritika*, Bilbao: Labayru Ikastegia, 2000.

Imaz, Eli. *Mujeres gestantes, madres en gestación. Representaciones, modelos y experiencias en el tránsito a la maternidad de las mujeres vascas contemporáneas*. Ph.D. Dissertation, UPV/EHU (University of the Basque Country), 2007.

Lasarte, Gema. *Pertsonaia protagonista femeninoen ezaugarriak eta bilakaera euskal narratiba garaikidean*. Ph.D. Dissertation, EHU/UPV (University of the Basque Country), 2011.

Olaziregi, Mari Jose. *Intimismoaz haraindi: Emakumezkoek idatzitako euskal literatura*. Oihenart 17. Donostia-San Sebastián: Eusko Ikaskuntza, Donostia, 1999.

Redondo Goicoechea, Alicia. *Jóvenes narradoras de los noventa*. Madrid: Narcea, 2003.

Rojo, Javier. *Egungo euskal ipuingintzaren historia*. Bilbao:

EHU/UPV (University of the Basque Country), 2011.

Urkiza, Ana. *Zortzi unibertso, zortzi idazle.* Irun: Alberdania, 2006.

Zerilli, Linda M. G. "A Process without a Subject: Simone de Beauvoir and Julia Kristeva on Maternity." *Signs* 18, No. 1 (Autumn, 1992): 111–35.

AURELIA ARKOTXA

Baigorri, Nafarroa Beherea, 1953

*A*urelia Arkotxa is a writer, professor, and researcher and lives in basque Atlantic Coast (Hendaye-Hendaia) since her childood. She holds a Hispanic Philology degree from the Université Bordeaux Montaigne (UBM) and is a doctor in Basque Philology. Her thesis was titled: *Imaginaire et poésie dans Maldan Behera de Gabriel Aresti 1933–1975*, and was published by ASJU in 1993. Today she teaches Basque philology and the classics at the campus of Nive, in the Département of Basque Studies (UBM-UPPA). She has conducted research on important figures in twentieth-century Basque literature include Aresti, Lete, Mirande, Lizardi, and others, she specializes in literature and history of Basque printing during the sixteenth and seventeenth centuries and is now working on new theories regarding *Linguae Vasconum Primitiae*.

In poetry she has published *Atari Ahantziak* (1993) *Septentrio* in Basque (2001), an adaptation and rewriting of *Septentrio* in French (2006) and *Septentrio* in Spanish (2007). Under the title *Fragmentuak* (2009) she has published a collection of her weekly poetry chronicles which were printed in the "Maratila" (2004–2014) section of the *Berria* newspaper, and in electronic press Kazeta.info (2014). She is member of the poetic movement "géopoétique".

In 2007 she was named a full member of the Royal Academy of the Basque Language. She was became the academy's vice president (January 2010–December 2012).

Cordelia

*K*ing Lear must divide his kingdom among his three daughters based on how much love each professes for him. The two eldest proclaim their great love for him by shouting, in an attempt to outdo one another. The third, Cordelia, remains silent. King Lear fails to see the love his youngest daughter feels for him and, sadly, splits his entire kingdom between his other two daughters. In 1913, Freud interpreted the story of King Lear and his three daughters by explaining that the story is about the choice this man has to make between three women. The fact that the man is a father is meaningless to the story. It is just his age that gives him the appearance of being their father. Let's continue with Shakespeare. In *The Merchant of Venice* Portia has three suitors. Who should she chose? She decides: she will present three small caskets to each suitor, one made of gold, one made of silver, and one made of lead. She hides her portrait in one of them. The first two men argue incessantly, one for the golden casket and the other for the silver. The third one chooses the leaden one, the casket that holds Portia's portrait. That is the man Portia will chose. This presents the counter argument of that of King Lear interpreted by Freud too. The three caskets symbolize three women or the idea of Womanhood. But they also represent the three Moira, three periods of time. The three Parca who keep spinning. The three deities of fate: Lachesis, Atropos, Clotho. They might also be the three representations of motherhood that a man will encounter throughout his life: his mother, lover, and mother earth. This last one "the Goddess of death, Death, the last one to embrace men" remains silent, like Cordelia.

Word Stalactites

"Trotting, trotting our lord is coming," "One mountain thirsty for water, another hungry for grass," "Strike while the iron is hot," I heard them all from my mother, who, similarly, heard them from her mother and she from her mother and grandmother. Mother says that proverbs flow naturally, that they can't be forced upon speakers, that people use them because "they want to say something," "because something has happened to them in life." They come from time immemorial. In order to reach great-grandmother, I would need to go all the way back to the mid-nineteenth century. Back in time. It's enough to follow the path of proverbs that we have received assembled in the Bible all the way from Solomon's or from the wisdom of ordinary people. They all work like kitchen recipes for life. Let's continue to go back in time. Great-grandmother's grandmother also passed along old proverbs as her mother and grandmother did. Now we are all the way back to about the era of Regent Egiategi who happened to love proverbs. We are at the beginning of the eighteenth century. Pushing time a little further, we meet Axular and Ionnes Etxeberri Ziburukoa, who considered proverbs to be of great significance and Oihenart, a collector of proverbs, who published two books in 1657 and 1665. And later, in 1596, we find *Refranes y sentencias*. Pascal Quigard states that "from the wall of time in which language has gradually hardened, proverbs fall, drop by drop, as people draw their mouths near." In his work, *Aspaldikoaz* (*Sur le jadis*, 2002) he also comments that proverbs are "precious stalactites" which have formed falling drop by drop from the wall of time.

Kaki Tree

*I*n wintertime, it stands like a miracle in the garden. Long, slender, leafless, and yet full of orange-colored fruit. They say that it is thought of as sacred in Japan and that they held it in great esteem in ancient Greece. For me, it is the tree of paradise. As, in October and November the tree gets covered with little round suns, it becomes a preferred meeting place for the neighborhood's blackbirds, song thrushes, turtle-doves, and magpies. Migratory birds know that the tree is in our garden, as if they spot it and target it from above. In my opinion, they must have already passed the word on to each other. A cloud of birds dives down and instantly covers the tree branches. The birds start eating until they feel satisfied. At this beginning of November, even the lonely birds that have fallen behind know where to replenish their strength. The tree welcomes them all, "onto her lap." I must say . . . yes, the male tree that I began writing about in my first lines has been turned into a female by my quill pen, into a mother. Mother, a source of life: good-hearted, peaceful, indolent. As soon as they feel satisfied, the delayed migratory birds quickly take off. They continue, again, on the journey in which they put their lives at risk. The rest will endure the winter here. They whistle and make a racket under the already languid

winter sun. With a quick blow from their beaks, they pierce
the thick orange skin and, overcome by gluttony, they extract
the pulpy chunks of fruit. Their eyes gleam as they swallow
the sweet flesh. It tastes like divine nectar to them. On the
bare tree, the fruit-loaded-branches droop like breasts full
of milk.

Stabat Mater

Once again I thought of the song's thread. Margarita and the other women are on their way to the river with baskets full of clothes. The current rinses the blood off Bereterretxe's shirts. The women's songs have reawakened the death of Mariasanz's son. The one that happened at night. Word has it that they hung him from the branches of the oak tree in Ezpeldoi. The tree still stands there, on the slope in the meadow, near the road. As they took her son a prisoner by force, as the count of Maule and his dark soldiers' horses trotted away, Mariasanz knew they would kill her son. Nevertheless, willing to save him, she hurried to her brother Buztanobi. Her brother did nothing. Mariasanz left. She hurried, hurried. From mountain to mountain. Up the hills, down the hills all the way to the castle in Maule. The count of Maule pointed his finger toward the mountains and informed her that her son was there, on the summit of Ezpeldoi and that she might be able to resurrect her dead son . . . he said laughing. That dreadful night, when the count and his soldiers surrounded the house, Bereterretxe told his mother: "Mother, give me a shirt, perhaps the last one I will ever wear. Those who remain alive will never forget the day after Easter." For he knew. The song ends there. Yet we know that Mariasanz went to Ezpeldoi and that her son's body lay there. For an instant, like Bramantino's Pietá, she held her dead son's head softly. The ballad, mentioning the day after Easter, signals that Bereter-retxe, like Christ, did not die. That he resurrected. Thanks to the clothes-washing song. He remains alive.

By Car

*J*ean Etxepare and six friends are off in a car early in the
morning. They plan to spend the day touring the Basque
Country. They are driving along looking for a place to have
lunch. They see small mountains on the north, wheat fields.
Finally, close to the village of Irurtzun, they find the shade
they longed for. The oak forest spreads its shade all the way
to the road. They stop the car. They find the perfect place
under a sweet shade. On the other side of the road an imposing farmhouse, with its windows wide open. While they are
eating, three children walk up to them. One of the travelers
asks them if they would like a piece of cake. The travelers
break into conversation in Basque with the grandmother
who is nearby. She tells them about how they thresh wheat
using yoked cows to trample the sheaves and how people in
the next town have contributed and bought a mechanical
thresher. She has her doubts about that new way of threshing
wheat. The travelers realize the children have not touched
the cake: "Children, have some cake and here some peaches
and pears too." But the children do not move and do not eat
anything. "They don't understand." Grandmother explains
that although their parents speak Basque, the children do not

know a single word in Basque. "*Comed,*" Grandmother says to the children and as they begin eating the cake they save a piece "*para la mamá.*"

UXUE APAOLAZA LARREA
Hernani, 1981

*U*xue Apaolaza Larrea, originally from Hernani, holds a degree in history, and has published two books: *Umeek gezurra esaten dutenetik* (From when children told lies, 2005), a collection of short stories, *Mea Culpa,* a novel 2011. For many years she has been a daily and weekly columnist in the Basque-language newspaper *Berria.* She has also worked with another Basque newspaper, *Argia,* and the Basque radio station, Euskadi Irratia, among others.

Iratxe Gutierrez Retolaza (see introduction) commented that Uxue Apaolaza Larrea's first book showcases an innovative style and a defined personality as well as a ruthless, sharp tone. According to Retolaza, furthermore, these stories do not make the readers feel judgmental or like merciful mothers (to mention two common moods in our storytelling tradition.) The stories trigger questions in our minds: "What if I / you / we were liars, evil, blameworthy, responsible?"

The Shopping Cart

She inserts the euro that she had ready in her pocket along with her visa card and keys into the coin slot. She advances slowly while checking her shopping list. She steers the cart with her left hand and right knee. She stops abruptly with a blank look. That music. It sounds like a song they used to sing in her youth. Her jeans fit her quite snugly, as is fashionable. When she walks, the car keys in her pocket dig at her a bit, more than the keys really, the keychain. Her husband bought it for her. A piece of junk.

She's been coming to this supermarket for years, ever since her first daughter was born and they bought their apartment in the neighborhood. At first she came with him. She still gets lost. There is always something that she cannot find. Salt, for example. She needs cereal for her daughter, the chocolate kind, it must be Kellogg's; the other kind gets soggy easily. Jam (sugar free) and butter for her husband. Sliced bread, whole wheat, for her other daughter, plus oranges and sliced ham. The cart can fill up fast but she still has lots of room.

Milk. Everyone drinks milk, though her husband needs the fat free kind (doctor's orders), her oldest daughter needs soymilk (the other kind causes an allergic reaction) and the fresh, daily kind for her youngest. She can't find the salt, and, besides, the key chain is hurting her. It's a duck. Made of hard plastic. They laughed when he gave it to her as a gift.

She parked the car a long distance away. Thankfully, she can walk all the way there pushing the shopping cart. Olive oil. She needs to buy scouring pads because the one in the bathroom is old and the kitchen one is not much better. The spinach looks good. She can make a puree for tonight. Her youngest daughter doesn't like it; it's all right, she'll fix something else for her (an omelet or fried eggs). She needs both hands now to steer the cart. Yogurt: for each their specific flavor, texture, brand. She wonders if it took her husband longer than a minute to select the keychain. No way. The biggest one, the more colorful the better, and now the duck's beak was poking her groin.

Chocolate, lentils, couscous, cheese: where's the cheese? Tomatoes, toothpaste, potatoes. Thinking of having to put everything away in the cupboards makes her feel tired. She wonders if she will have enough strength. She doesn't like the smell of the fish market. The fish counter at the supermarket doesn't smell as bad but doesn't smell much better. Fish is expensive enough already but she must buy the most expensive kind. Almost. And shrimp. For tomorrow. Fresh, of course. Her daughters do not like fish (except shrimp), and tuna. She'll need to throw a third of what she buys in the trash. She takes her sweater off and leaves it inside the cart. President. Her youngest daughter likes that brand of Camembert cheese. She smiles and scratches her head. President. She leaves it there, on the white shelf.

She sees the frozen shrimp, in big bags and takes one, in fear. She can serve them that tomorrow instead of the fresh kind. She laughs picturing her daughters' faces. Frozen croquettes, French fries, a potato omelet! Canned soup. Pound cake wrapped in shiny paper, the kind that one eats desperately. Ketchup and hotdogs (filled with cheese, ham flavored). She bursts into laughter once again. They would not let her in the house. Coca-Cola. Yes, she should get some. Her youngest added it to the list at the last minute, "Don't forget it, eh!" Her oldest daughter will scold her for giving money to a criminal multinational. Her head hurts and her groin too.

She stops in front of the chocolate-bar section. So many colors. She takes one. Golden. Made with caramel and cookies, and it tastes delicious. She takes another one in exchange for the euro she used earlier to get the shopping cart, and takes off.

She leaves the shopping cart full of groceries, the wrapping of the chocolate-bar she just ate and the plastic key chain in front of the chocolate display. No farewell letter. Farewell letters often contain nothing but lies; if the truth were to be written in them, no one would understand it anyway.

In the Family

*A*fter Mother helped me settle into my wheelchair, I held on tightly to the safety bar that Father installed for me in the back of the van. I looked eagerly at the open road before me. "Faster, Mother, faster!" I screamed to my mother every time she got behind the steering wheel. Mother always looked at me through the rearview mirror and, with the typical grin of many mothers and wives, shook her head, no.

This situation always frightened Mother. That is what I believed then. I should still believe it now but you will understand later why I'm not that certain of it anymore. My mother overcame that fear every week to please me, because she believed that her daughter's laughter was worth it, and also, I know this because she told me, because it took two days before the anger I felt toward the world returned; and that meant a lot when it came to my interaction with people. I only interacted with Mother. "Let's not over do it," she told me time after time, not wishing to see her daughter, wheelchair and all, thrown into the middle of the road.

That day turned out to be, how should I say, special. That Saturday, Mother got up in good spirits for the first time since leaving Father. At first she used to get up in a sour mood, and lately, gloomy. As her mood transformed from sour to gloomy, her driving got slower. And as for me, I wanted her to go faster. That is why I preferred Mother to be in a good or even in a sour mood instead of the gloomy state she had been in for the last few months.

I heard the motor turn over; my muscles tensed, especially my stomach muscles. We took off slowly so I would not injure the muscles in my arm. I screamed. I don't recall distinctly the exact moment because I release the same scream every weekend. It would have been easier to recall a moment when I had not screamed. Nevertheless, I am sure that I did scream. I thought of American movies where the youngsters going on a road trip, driving a convertible, blend their screams with the first chords of a Beach Boys song. That was exactly what I did from the back of the van. *UuuuuUUUU! UU! UUUU!!!!!!!* Something like that. I felt butterflies in my stomach.

The van began to speed up. The elderly, who strolled down the sidewalks, smiled at me. Mother would quit flooring the accelerator soon and we would drive at an even speed the rest of the way, allegro, you know. I am not very exact when I say that because, really, I felt we were driving faster than usual. I was thrilled and screamed for a second time. I recall this second scream very vividly; for example, I know that I screamed with my eyes closed because I never screamed twice on weekends. I thought it was great that Mother was in a good mood, until I began to feel nervous.

"Mother that's enough! Will you slow down?" It was the first time I made such a request. I did not like it. Not one bit. Mother was ruining the game. Our routine went down the drain. I was supposed to ask for more speed and then Mother was supposed to refuse my request with that typical mothers' grin. That little argument was vital for my self-esteem. For one, it created a rebellious spirit in me that all youth need to feel; it is not good to feel that your mother is more progressive and daring than you. And two, believing that my mother would not put my life at risk for a transitory moment of happiness was reassuring. A mother has the biological responsibility to protect her daughter. Even more, to super protect her!

My stomach churned. Unlike other times, Mother had her window rolled all the way up. "Don't worry, this damn road must end somewhere," I thought. I cursed the road. Can you believe it? I cursed my only source of happiness and it was my mother's fault. I tried closing my eyes and taking deep breaths but I could not.

Mother loved me yet her behavior didn't seem like it. The episode could have traumatized me, actually, it did. And that is when I realized all this could just be a trick. Mother could be fed up with this weekend anxiety and routine. She could have decided to give me a scare because she could not put up with the tension our quips created. This hurt me, though. I was no longer a child in need of this type of lesson. I can't find the words now to describe the intensity of the pain I felt then because the fright that overcame me later made that first feeling seem insignificant in comparison. But I'm certain that at the time the pain had not been insignificant at all.

My arm was getting tired—the physical and psychological tensions were too much to handle at once—my knuckles were turning cold, my fingers hurt. I felt the urge to cry. I remember clearly the urge to cry out of helplessness, of anger. She had not lifted her foot off the gas pedal since she had started the van. The roaring of the motor was frightening.

I believe that at the very moment I felt that urge to cry, I began to doubt my mother's love for me. This is an excru-

ciating feeling for any daughter. Though in time the feeling
might dissipate, just having it cross your mind is excruciating. I will repeat it: excruciating. Perhaps she did love me, I
thought. But did she love me enough to spend her entire day
taking care of me? I began punishing myself, as if the mere
fact of having such thoughts were not enough punishment. I
am not a very autonomous girl. After the accident, I turned
into even more of a loner than I had been before the accident; Mother was the only one who acknowledged me, more
than I acknowledged myself, really. It is still the case. I never
showed her my appreciation. It was her job, as I mentioned
earlier, she held the biological responsibility . . . It was as obvious as ever. I had never verbalized it, "it's your responsibility," but that is how we acted, as if my handicap were her
responsibility. I believed that we both shared that belief.

Will any of the readers understand my anger toward life?
I am such an unfortunate person; life has betrayed me, and
those who surround me embody my frustration. That morning her good mood made me happy, just because of the speed,
that was all—you can't ask me to feel happy for someone
else's good mood when I am so unfortunate—and as usual
I lashed out at her. I recall, word for word, how I welcomed
her when she entered the room, singing, bringing me a cup
of coffee with milk. I still remember it well because of the
string of words that flooded my mind when I was in the back
of the van: "Shit, why me? Why does the world ignore my
misfortune? And you, Mother, you are the one who ignores
it most. What time is it? Answer my question, Mother. What
time is it? I see, ten thirty. Didn't we agree that you would
bring me breakfast at ten? I've been waiting half an hour for
you, half an hour! Do you know what that means? Do you realize this means that my schedule is completely upside down

today? My routine is not in my hands but yours and you don't
seem to realize the extent of the pain it causes me, each time
you show this lack of concern because it reminds me of my
incapacity to do things on my own and, furthermore, to correct your mess-ups. You haven't chosen to have a crippled
daughter, but do you think it was my choice to have a dumb
mother? Don't social services mention anything about that?
Anything about crippled daughters who have to put up with
dumb mothers? It takes a minimum of intelligence to step
into the shoes of those of us who live in misfortune and I'm
not sure you even try, and if you do, obviously, you don't try
hard enough."

I realized that I had acted selfishly; that I acted selfishly
every day. I was ready to make an effort, but truth be told,
there are ways and there are ways to say things. The roaring
of the motor was deafening. We were going fast. I believe she
was no longer flooring the accelerator, but still, the danger
was obvious, obvious indeed!

The back of the van was not the best place to think, and
yet, all kinds of thoughts darted through my little head. If
Mother was fed up and her anger had reached this level, it
did not match her great mood today. She spoke louder today.
My disrespectful comments did not sour her mood. She did
not sip her coffee with milk while gazing at the cup. She suddenly hugged me and gave me little kisses. She was not really kissing me but rather herself. That outburst of happiness
was self-contained; it did not have anything to do with me.
Perhaps, after Father left, she was thrilled to make her own
decisions, but there was something slowing her down—me. I
felt my blood freeze. Literally, I believe my blood froze.

The speed, the window, she put aside her characteristic,
crash-avoiding driving. I could imagine her, with her pale

complexion, standing before the judge. She would not need to make much of an effort to make her case because she looks so pitiful. When she bows her head, she adopts such a pitiful voice, each word channeled between her teeth.

"Your Honor, I do recognize my negligence and I am ready to accept responsibility but, please be honest: how can a mother rob her daughter of the only thing that makes her happy? At one point in her life my daughter, was a red-cheeked girl that ran free on the green fields of Euskal Herria. It broke my heart to see her sit in her wheelchair pleading to us. We always drove carefully but that day, a moment of euphoria seized me; our eyes locked in the rearview mirror, we became one, your Honor, and we were flying over the asphalt, disregarding the exhaust. It just happened, but I can assure you that my daughter died happy, though the sight was somewhat grotesque." Satisfied? Oh my, dear reader, I have never felt so miserable, so defenseless. To have to die feeling furious! I envisioned very distasteful headlines, which hurt my self-esteem deeply.

When I was about to give up, when I felt I was going to die in that nightmare because I decided to let go of the safety-bar, to let what was going to happen, happen, such was my despair, I felt the van slowing down. We were reaching the end of the road. I relaxed, though not completely. I knew this episode would change my life. Had she wanted to, she could have killed me by merely slamming on the brakes.

At last we stopped. I felt as if all my muscles had died at once. Only my heart remained in motion and that involuntary trembling was not able to jump-start my muscles. Gushing tears and snot.

The door opened and I realized at once that the one getting out of the van was not Mother. For starters, it was a man, a blond man. "Where is my mother? What did you do to her you son of a bitch! I knew Mother did not want to kill me, I knew it! Do you hear me, you son of a bitch? I knew it! What do you want to do to me? Do you want to rape this cripple who can't wipe her own ass? That's what you want? Just say it! Is that what you want?" I told him all that.

My parents hoped to surprise me (and they sure did). After the letter Father sent Mother, they were once again together. How sweet. *Father and Mother sitting in a tree . . .* That had been the reason why Father wanted to drive the van that day, so he could feel a part of the family once again, and that is why Mother let him do it—*k-i-s-s-i-n-g*—so he would drive faster. They were hoping I would share their renewed happiness instead of screaming my lungs out like a hysteric paranoiac, not realizing that the man standing before me was my own father. I'm sorry, but you should have warned me.

MAITE GONZALEZ ESNAL

Donostia, 1943

What an odd "pedestal" that of motherhood. Herds of voices whisper incessantly:

"Mother I'm no longer the child in the photo snuggling on your lap."
"I've grown and moved away from the photo to live to the edge of a cliff."
"Listen, Mother: I hid everything from you so you would not bear more stones in your heart."
"Thank you, Mother: I owe you language that you fed me word by word like porridge."
"But, where are you, Mother? At nighttime, sheets give me chills. Please, tuck me in under the covers!"
"I don't want your courage; you can keep it for yourself! What law ordered you to guard my womb?"

My dear children: we are nothing but women,
As fragile as Ischnura elegans, dragonflies,
Trying to protect our wings when falling from the pedestal. That's all.

He Wanted to Clip Her Wings

*I*t might be that I do not know the meaning of the word craving; for that reason, I did what ignorant people should do: I turned to the book of books. Still, it was no use. On the contrary, the dictionary left me lost amid a forest of ethics and morality. It says that cravings are wrong, something excessive. Depending on who the author of the dictionary is, they can even turn out to be sinful.

I am aware that my problem might be a personal one, a kind of psychological punishment of some sort or a tax that I am obligated to pay for being a woman that has not matched the generosity of Madonnas; because apparently craving, that irrational urge, is attached to motherhood, to be more precise, to pregnancy.

The fact that I haven't known the bewilderment of the Madonnas' doesn't blind me. Let me turn to the family dictionary, to those unwritten words that express love and hate and get passed down from generation to generation; to the dictionary within the home.

I heard the word craving for the first time from my father's lips, when he referred to Mother's whims as something connected to femininity. He used to say jokingly that Mother's cravings had to be satisfied, and he was not the only one who thought that. If one of my uncles happened to be around when Father said that, the uncle would nod in agreement. Sometimes, for no other reason than perpetuating the oral tradition, the uncle would repeat for the thousandth time one of Grandfather's sayings in order to hold on to old beliefs. Not necessarily because Mother had a tendency to crave but because Father, as a man who held on tightly to tradition, two or three times a year would try hard to satisfy the cravings that he supposed Mother had. Because manhood in itself requires satisfying a gift-giving quota without accounting for whom the gift is intended. The craving-offering altar was in the kitchen. We children did not dare eat from it because it had been brought expressly for Mother, though she yearned for something different. However, they both ate from it: Father ate solemnly because it was a once-a-year ritual. Mother on the other hand ate with conflicted sentiments, a captive of conventionalism. She had to act thankful because it was a gift but hide her frustration at all cost while her real wish got lost amid theater curtains; her wings clipped so she would not travel through her fiction. However, when we least expected, inspired by the wounds in her wings, she showed us the crocodile inside her, crying here and showing her teeth there.

It is indeed very uncomfortable to see to what an extent resignation transforms us into worn-out users of language. Every spring Mother lashed out against the sack of *ziza* mushrooms saying, "what a mediocre kind of mushroom." Then, Father would take the small knife in his hand and start chopping onions. Instead of joining his friends at the men's *txoko* he would stay home to have dinner with her. To this day the disdain Mother feels toward that kind of mushrooms persists; I don't mind it. I respect this feeling as I respect the faith she puts in chamomile.

It is dreadful how heavy the burden of traditions can be. Mother's behavior was quite different toward the *kuleto*, the king of all mushrooms. She always said that to celebrate Santa Ana's day, with the assistance of the moon, her family home never lacked a great tray of *kuleto*s roasted in the oven, sprinkled with garlic and parsley. But since Father's San Prudenzio day was always celebrated with *zizak* those two gastronomic biographies stayed separate like the Muslims' lamb and the Protestants' pork; remaining enemies, never intermingling.

What happened with barnacles was metaphysical. She felt an atavistic fear toward them. She lost one of her relatives on the coastal rocks of Jaizkibel while he was looking for them. The rough sea prevented finding his body for an entire week and, since then, she thought of the risk as unnecessary, foolish, and it goes without saying, she saw barnacles as terrifying bearers of death.

I remember the "craving day" when they would sit at the kitchen table facing each other in a tender mood. Mother dared to cast the line: "I heard on the radio that a Zarzuela is coming to town." Reply: a barnacle-slurping noise.

Mother did not complain. She was ignored but she still had her Zarzuela to hold onto. One day she would have the opportunity to do as she pleased, like when she had a chance to vote for the Republic.

I went back to the dictionary. It also lists "Will," followed by "Desire" and other nouns and adjective combinations. Of course my intention is not to upset the authors of dictionaries, not at all. I don't blame them for Father's shortsightedness either. I know well that language is a web where one gets trapped and that because we betray dictionaries constantly, they are worthless. But who will write a dictionary for those who come after my father so it will cure their blindness and make them see reality?

EIDER RODRIGUEZ

Errenteria, 1979

*E*ider Rodriguez holds a degree in advertising and has published many articles in newspapers. Currently she is a professor at the University of the Basque Country in the Department of Language and Literature.

Rodriguez has published three short story collections that have been very well received. *Eta handik gutxira gaur* (And soon there after now, 2004), *Haragia* (Flesh, 2007*)*, *Katu jendea* (Cat people, 2010). The first two have been translated into and published in Spanish and the third one has been published in five different languages.

As Iratxe Retolaza stated in a review for the feminist criticism website *Sareinak* on February 2, 2008, Eider Rodriguez provides information in small and measured doses. She offers the reader many characters' worldviews by using a lyric-cynical and melancholy tone. She achieves it all through the power and sharpness of narration.

She translated Irene Nemirovsky's *Le bal* into Basque (2006).

The Seed

*I*t's already been five months since he was born. I'm at the window smoking a cigarette. Half of my body leaning out and the other half glued to the kitchen floor—the metaphor of my existence. Even though they tell me, after taking a step back and fixing their eyes on my waist, that I've regained my pre-pregnancy figure, I'm not the same. I know that and everyone else knows it too. I'm no longer the same.

Until five months ago, though my womb was about to burst, though my feet and lips were swollen, though I had lost my waistline long before, I still got job offers and other kinds too. I was on the market, a negotiable commodity. People continued cultivating me, some by offering me imaginary jobs, others inviting me out to coffee, sharing projects with me they hadn't shared with anyone else . . . Any day could be harvest time and, perhaps, that little seed: the job offer, the coffee, the invitation to the concert, would grow to become a beautiful plant. The ways of seduction are always mysterious.

Now I'm left fallow, as if I were a defective product; now, when I have more time than ever to go out for coffee and listen to job offers; now, that I have recovered not only my waist but also the ability to roll over in bed without the help of a crane, I hear handfuls of seed falling on other's soil and rusty sprinklers turning under the sun.

I'm a pariah. Unmentionable. Untouchable. They don't utter my name nor dial my phone number, even accidentally. As parents lay it on their children, so the world lays its prohibition over me: "Do not touch," or "if you want to try her out, please ask a salesperson first."

I feel as if I live surrounded by diplomats, except these don't wear ties, but rather dress in "Pull and Bear" clothing, and speak only two languages, poorly. The diplomats initiate the protocol as soon as they see me; "How's the little one?" "You must be so busy," "How old is he already?" "Is he good?" "Does he let you sleep at all?" Answers that don't matter to anybody but me. They don't look me in the eye and sometimes they even ask me the same question twice, at times walking away before I get to finish answering. They get swept away by life's current and barely get enough time to wave a white handkerchief when saying goodbye. I'm the one who remains behind, smoking a cigarette, in this place where nothing happens.

I'm only good for satisfying the basic, physiological needs of others. I'm like a cow, a mediocre cook, a hooker who has known better days. Functional like a blender. Press here and I start up. Predictable, submissive, average. No one waits for me, at least not with anticipation and excitement. I'm like a fly.

Another cigarette smoked by my outward half while I look out the window. There, on that side, only leaves and used Kleenex move. To be fair, that smashed tomato left lying in the middle of the road deserves to be included because decomposing things are moving too. Here, on the inside, the sheets; the sheets are the only moving things. The clock. The refrigerator. This half who lives inward has often hugged the shivering refrigerator; it's so appreciative and of such good size, it makes me feel so protected while the baby is asleep.

It's time for him to wake up, but I still have time to smoke another cigarette. Three cigarettes in fourteen months, that's nothing.

Though I'd like to keep my head and eyes far away from here, I'm a split woman whose roots are strongly held fast to the ground. My feet are suction cups, while the other half of my body outside the window longs to fly away. Since I gave birth, I have not healed. And what is worse, I don't think I ever will. I'm a chronic case.

But I don't pose any danger. I'm not dangerous anymore. Not to anyone. Everyone knows where I am and where I'll be during the next twelve hours, twelve days, twelve years. Everyone knows who I'm with and what keeps me up at night.

The only danger would be for me to get depressed; to get depressed and frighten everyone. The woman who placed her baby in the washing machine, the man who left his twins baking inside the car in the dead of August, all those television features generating sympathy for me in the minds of my family and friends when they ask me "how are you, dear?" That is one of the few openings I have left to be dangerous.

My husband should be here by now. He's late today, again.

We finally got married, trying to show absolute normality, perhaps, I'm not sure. It wasn't a very well thought-out decision: it wasn't too exciting, but it didn't bother us too much either. We had a discreet wedding. After the reception, my husband and I went to watch a movie, perhaps needing to feel we were still the same as before. It was lovely.

Thirteen years later I'm no longer sure if I live with my husband or my brother. We bought this house . . . He did . .

. They did . . . His parents did. When we got married. In exchange every Sunday, we need . . . I need . . . to put up with
them . . . With his mother. The old man watches the handball
game with my husband. Sometimes he also takes a nap in
front of the television . . . They do. She and I talk about all
the remodeling that could be done to the house in the future:
enclosing the terrace with windows to gain a room, adding
a bathroom in case the family grows in the future, avoiding
lines to defecate or masturbate. Of course, this last comment
goes unsaid.

This way you won't need to pay a mortgage, they told us .
. . she told me . . . his mother, when we were looking at houses. You may be able to quit your job, she said, while checking
the sturdiness of a wall, knocking on it with her knuckles.
Let's get out of here. This house is made of chocolate, she
concluded. My husband and my father-in-law were checking
the seal on the windows.

And I did. I quit working, that is, but not because I wanted to, but because others wanted me to. Not my mother-
in-law but the other others. Since I became pregnant, they
wouldn't even call me to play the part of a pregnant woman.
They would rather use a flawless, touchable, mentionable
woman with a polyester pillow. No luck after the delivery either: to play the role of mother it was enough to apply a little
blush to one of those pre-pubescent girls.

It has been a little over a year since I got my last role in
a film. Professionally, it has been the most important part I
have ever played: a taxidermist's assistant. Though, at first,
it is a secondary role, toward the end it turns into a more
prominent role, when it gets disclosed that she sedates people and takes their eyes out with a teaspoon, for placement in
the animals' sockets. This is not a role that an actress dreams

of, I'm not that naïve. But until that point, I had only played a nurse, a lover, a friend, a classmate, a cousin, and an aerobics instructor. Playing the taxidermist assistant made me think that I was done being the tinsel on the Christmas tree. I was wrong. I'm always wrong, without fail.

My fourth cigarette. Everything is so quiet that I can hear the paper burning. I had forgotten that Marlboros tasted like caramel.

The baby will wake up anytime now, he's resting sweetly. Someday he too will see me as a mother, a nameless, generic mother.

Sometimes it makes me sad to watch him sleeping. "You smell like a mother," a wannabe film director told me this morning. "And what is that smell like?" I asked him. "I'm not sure, like a muffin," he answered. He told me that I looked beautiful, that I have new little freckles on my nose and that he will call to offer me one of those imaginary jobs when he is not so busy. Obviously, this last note is my own. He approached the baby and, stretching out his arm, barely moving his body, as if there were some radioactive material underneath, he lifted the blanket. Then he kissed me half way between my ear and my lips. "Take care." As if I did not have anything better to do. He left in a hurry.

Before the delivery, there was nothing between us, but there was the possibility of maybe-something-someday that, on one hand, kept me from falling asleep when listening to his projects and on the other, made him talk to me about his projects with great detail and conviction. Later, much later, after the cups got cold, we would hug each other goodbye with the promise that soon we would get together to have a longer coffee, perhaps that same week or the next. And the echo of that longer coffee lingered in the air, sometimes turning into a quickie session against the wall, other times into a nervous and intense kiss, though we never called each other to verify the seriousness of that promise. But every time we met, the eroticism between us recharged. Until the delivery. More than desirable, I felt meaningful. Perhaps that is the difference between then and now, between here and there. Now, here, I am only meaningful for my son. In the words of that wannabe director, I emanate a muffin-like smell.

It is not just about fornicating. Sex is not the issue, the same as when buying a house the issue is not the sturdiness of the walls or the tightness of the window seals. The issue is value, how much am I worth, where am I located, who else lives in the neighborhood, and who wants to buy me. That is how they set the criteria for selection. It is based on the desire of others. And everything else is a lie. Or at least, it is not true.

Houses, storefronts, actors, actresses, sausages, and me. I live hoping that that guy or someone like him will invite me to do something. I recognize it. I do not think of the mercenary aspect anymore. From now on I will not be hired, I will be invited only if, other than close relatives, there is anyone on the face of the earth that has not erased my number from their cell phone. Well-educated, well made-up and even better dressed, I am a good candidate to be invited. After applying the last dab of perfume, and as soon as I go out, I would like to shout to the world that I belong in this party too, that I'm not out of place and that I would be a bargain when it came to the cost of food and drink, therefore, economical; economical and beautiful.

I lost track of my friends a long time ago. Besides, no one, except other mothers and children, enjoy spending time with mothers.

My husband should be here any time. My mother says

that they look identical. His mother says it too, every single time. A lie that women have repeated century after century to put to rest any doubt about the legitimacy of a child and, therefore, to protect the mother and the offspring from being murdered or abandoned by the husband.

The species has been able to endure thanks to lies. He will arrive, and it will take him ten minutes before realizing his son is in the next room. He forgets about him. They say that fathers do not become fully aware of their fatherhood until the child turns two.

I'm not eager to see him come home, but I'm anticipating his arrival. His face will contort when he sees me smoking. Or he may not even notice, who knows. He might have forgotten that I was an ex-smoker up until this morning.

The baby should have awakened by now. I always check that the sheet moves lightly around his abdomen, that he's alive, that I am still needed. He'll become like his father, a man who will keep someone like me next to him, someone who, like me, will wait for him, though, at the same time, not be eager to see him arrive.

I might still have enough time to smoke another cigarette before he wakes up.

Beauty is not the problem, because I'm still beautiful. The problem is that I'm no longer prey who can provoke a fight among hunters. Who's stupid enough to want to shoot a caged hare? Who wants to show off game hunted under such circumstances? That's no fun. Hunters want to play around, sniff here and there, listen to their dogs closely, feel the sweat before pulling the trigger, a shadow behind a blade of grass, nervous barking, lift the gun, close an eye and shoot: the smell of burnt plastic, the prey still pulsing, "That's the third one." Hunters can only admire their prey when comparing it to that of other hunters.

I can't deny that I feel cheated. Is this life? Is this it? Such a fuss for this? And still thirty, forty, fifty, sixty years ahead of me. Could anyone tell me what I need this much time for?

He's here. I can hear him, his way of walking ... His footsteps sound as if he has glue on the soles of his shoes. He's here. Please, could someone show him the way? He's never been very good in the dark.

A discreet applause for him too.

Good evening, my dear. How was your day? Here I am, nothing new to report, you know, the baby has finally pooped, that is what he needed, that is why he was so fussy, no doubt, a hard and black piece of poop. I meant to keep it, but I got rid of it; other than that, here, you know, nothing much. Your mother called. I guess your father's aunt is in the hospital and they went to visit her.

Ah, and they called from the garage to let you know you can go pick up the car.

But sit down, dear, sit down, tell us about your day. You may feel strange talking in front of so many people, but do not be shy, once you begin, it will be OK.

We saved a seat for you, for you and for your parents, but they won't be able to make it. Such a shame, for once they could have seen me working, in a modest venue, but nevertheless with a very personal script.

The play is almost over, dear. Would you like to come up and see your son? Not this one, this is the rubber one. I'm talking about the real one, the one back there, backstage.

MIREN AGUR MEABE

Lekeitio, 1962

*M*iren Agur Meabe studied Basque Philology and for many years worked in education and as a textbook author. She received the Critic Award in 2001 and 2011 for her volumes of poetry *Azalaren kodea* (The code of the skin) and *Bitsa eskuetan* (Foam in my hands). She also received the Euskadi Award on three occasions for her three young adult novels *Itsaslabarreko etxea* (The house on the cliff, 2002), *Urtebete itsasargian* (A year at the lighthouse, 2006), and *Errepidea* (The road, 2010).

Her work *Mila magnolia lore* (A thousand magnolias), in which she intertwines poetry and prose, was named to the 2012 IBBY List of Honour.

She has participated at different literature gatherings such as the Dublin Writers Festival in 2003, the XXI Vjlenica International Literary Festival in 2006, the Edinburgh International Book Festival in 2007, Cervantes Institute in Vienna in 2008, the University of California, Santa Barbara, the Center for Basque Studies at the University of Nevada, Reno in 2008, and the Frankfurt Book Fair in 2009.

Since 2006, she has been an associate member of Euskaltzaindia (the Royal Academy of the Basque Language).

Lilia's Pearls or How Doltza and Her Name Changed

*B*ecause those wild ducks that had fallen behind their flock upset me and the moonlight frightened me, I lit a small fire in an open field, afraid of getting cold. I lay down and cried.

I used to cry once in a while . . . but who doesn't?

I cried from exhaustion after forty days and nights of nonstop walking, pulling a cart that carried the chest with seven locks. I bought the cart, which, thankfully, is quite small, with the wages I received as payment for my first jobs. My voice was highly regarded at parties and celebrations, for which they used to hire me to sing verses and tell stories.

I cried from hunger after forty days and nights of fasting, eating only a few black plums and berries.

I cried from loneliness after forty days and nights of purposely not seeing anyone. Silence is a person's inner home, truly, and the word is its door but the words that remain imprisoned inside end up rotting the entrails and those few words that free themselves randomly are not always enough to heal the innards.

I knew that no one would pave my way.

For a while an owl kept gazing at me, until suddenly the moon darkened, thunder boomed and it began raining, pouring. Then, I had to get up to find shelter.

I noticed a spark of light peaking among the eucalyptus trees and I hastened there as my tired feet followed the rippling sound of the stream, which seemed to mimic a murmuring voice in the dark. The sound of the water took me all the way up to the door of a mill in front of which stood a young boy holding an oil lamp.

The scattered wisps of hay in the entrance of the house and the aroma of bread made me believe I had just arrived home, yet, I could not be farther from my birthplace. Paintings and tapestries covered the living room walls of the house.

A few children slept in cots and next to the hearth a woman nursed a child. The woman caught my attention because she was clearly older, and the child was not a baby. The woman said:

"Rest. My name is Lilia, Lilia Leakoa."

I made myself comfortable in a place where I could lie down while thinking that the woman had the perfect name for she was like the lilies in the fields but not necessarily because of her beauty. She was thin compared to me because I have a good-sized waist. Nevertheless, she had an air of elegance and a commanding disposition.

"You're wrong," she read my mind. "My name has nothing to do with flowers but with the wind and the night."

I quickly sensed that she was a confident woman.

I slept all night until some clatter woke me at sunrise. Lilia had to work hard to watch over so many children, half a dozen plus one. They were all so close to each other in age.

"They can all fend for themselves except for this poor one," she clarified, guessing once again what I was thinking. She was referring to the child she held on her lap the night before. Now she was in a crib, whining. "She was born crying and lives crying. She has an incurable disease in her brain. Who knows! The damned one has soured my breast milk," she uttered bitterly as she kicked the crib with her foot.

She offered me baked apples, honey, and white wine to break my fast.

"Eat and renew your strength. You'll stay, right?" And looking at her children she said, "Get out of here! Go to the convent and tell the nuns that Lilia sends you, that we have a guest, and to keep you for a few days."

I nodded. I felt like staying, because the need of company during the time I spent in the wilderness alone had become painful and because the woman had a kind of magnetism.

I observed the surroundings of the mill through the window. Reeds bowed, subdued to the winter wind gusts and hundreds of shells and mussels shone in the mud. Up from the swamp, a meadow splattered with gorse and rocks and on a circular corner a herd of horses grazed. The weather was poor.

"Who is in charge of the work at the mill? You?" I asked Lilia.

"No, I'm the one who had it built but I welcome anyone who wants to use it. In exchange, farmers offer me their help chopping wood or supply me beans. Fishermen help with what they can, a plateful of anchovies in spring and a chunk of tuna in summer."

She paused to ask me about my intentions, merely a polite gesture, since she answered the question herself.

"And what has brought you here? You are a special woman. It's obvious that you are eager for knowledge. But the mysteries of knowledge as well as those of love and luck remain hidden."

"I don't know exactly how I arrived here. The road

brought me to your home and whatever the road has to offer, I take."

"Then, you'll want to see now something you haven't seen lately. Come."

She ushered me to the library where crooked piles of books stood on the floor and tools and instruments lay on shelves. There was a human body on a table, preserved as if to be used to study its anatomy. There were dozens of papers rolled and tied up with strings on the shelves. And hanging on the walls there were diagrams of star constellations, animal skeletons, buildings, towns, gardens, and many other things.

"Do you know what this is?" She pointed at a drawing of a machine. "Apparently the inventor stated that it's an army of twenty six lead soldiers, which can conquer the world . . . the printing press. Well, the real inventors were the Chinese, a few centuries ago. They built it out of wood, but since it often broke down, it became impossible to disseminate many copies."

Lilia had a wide knowledge of art, astronomy, physics, architecture, music, medicine, and letters. But she despised politics:

"Disgusting laws, laws made by disgusting people," she grumbled. "Just think that, for example, in times of the witch hunt they were capable of killing six hundred women a year . . . religion and politics are nothing but the factory of our shadows!"

She taught me how to read and write, and that is why, if someone asked me today which is the most difficult form of art, I would never say that the art of reading and writing properly is inferior to any other form of art.

We worked hard together, especially at nighttime, tenaciously, without giving up when faced with challenges. We were surgeons when we had to be and teachers when called upon. From cutting and extracting small lumps from women's breast to taming young women's narcissistic behaviors, we did it all. We stuffed birds, sheep, monkeys, frogs, and badgers so we could compare their organs to those of humans. It became our challenge to feed the beggars that knocked on our door, to discuss the theories trumpeted by the know-it-alls or to extract from poets their best lines. Days went on at the mill while we kept testing and learning.

Although many people came to see Lilia, she was not free of being the subject of gossip. Some in town referred to her as the "old whore" and spat on the ground when we walked by.

At dawn, when the tide was down, we would go to the beach to rest. The sand would be embroidered with sandpipers' tracks, delicate prints with no specific direction, like my own path often.

With the water up to our chests we felt small red mullets, sea brims, catfish, and black breams brushing against our bodies and amid the coastal rocks we caught sea urchins to study later.

"Draw something in the sand," Lilia asked me once handing me her red handled cane. "Whatever comes to you."

I tried to draw the sun, a house, faces, and other things but I did not succeed because the sand was too dry.

"Often, to live is to make squiggles until the wave comes and leaves the sand ready," she said, once again answering my thoughts.

There was a painting in the house that I cherished, a self-portrait. It was of Lilia in the water surrounded by plants, birds, and fish, her legs wide open, with deep, purple creases on her belly and going through labor pains. Her vagina poured out seven pearls, seven big pearls, each resembling one another.

"Don't think that those pearls are my children. Let's see, tell me, how are pearls formed?"

"When a foreign body penetrates the oyster, the animal inside reacts by secreting a substance," I said, recalling what I had learned.

"Be more specific, please! Nacre, secreting nacre . . ."

"With time, layers of nacre cover the foreign object, until little by little the pearl is formed."

"You said it yourself: pearls are the result of the oyster's defense mechanism."

"Then, the pearls are the metaphors of suffering?"

"Not exactly, don't you get so dramatic, you even made a sad face. Let's say that there are seven laws, my seven treasures, those that life handed to me. You wonder how I've gotten them? Making the most of pain, controlling rage, and enjoying the pleasures at hand. And of course, holding onto my studies."

"And what are those seven pearls?"

"Listen carefully, since Lilia won't repeat her seven rules. . . First: care for nature and all its beings as you care about yourself. Second: love, without ever pronouncing the word *love*. Third: feed knowledge and cultivate your thoughts in your mind and your heart. Fourth: do not punish yourself continuously for your mistakes. Fifth: help the needy no matter if they are big or small. Sixth: accept sadness and responsibility, as if they were a link to well-being, but avoid dark shadows. Seventh: be loyal to your friends and keep their secrets and your word.

And after she had declared these rules, she held the shell

used by pilgrims and poured water on my head.

"From today on your name will be Doltza. Doltza, the sound of sweet water, so you feel whole."

That is how my teacher changed my name, which until then, had been Urria. She gave me a new name. And I changed too.

Once in a while men came to see Lilia looking for love-games. They would all ask her: "Do you like me? Do you like me?" and she would answer them pleased, laughing. It was obvious that she welcomed them willingly, without further commitment.

"Listen," she would tell me, "each child has a different father, and they carry only my last name. As you can see, no man lives in this house, I don't want any. There's no man that will keep me longing for him, nor will any man unexpectedly abandon me."

She and I lay together too whenever we pleased. Her embraces were for me more stimulating than sweet wine, and mine were for her more calming than mint-water.

"My silly one, I'll teach you everything I know," she promised me and she meant what she said.

I felt satisfied, her hair parted to the side, I blew, kissed or tickled her scales because her neck was covered in fish scales. The first time I noticed them, I pulled my hand away, in fear.

"Don't be afraid, you foolish one. Like Laminas who have kept their unique chicken, duck or goat feet, so I as a lover of water have kept my scales. Or in today's world, should we lose completely all our vestiges of the past?"

But when it came to dealing with the littlest one, Lilia acted harshly. That was her deep weakness: she would shake her, in desperation, and even pinch her. Even though I adored Lilia, every time I saw her act like that I would feel like I was drowning in a river of mud and in order to calm my fury, I would tell the child:

"If you quiet down, I'll tell you a story."

I would take her outside of the house and sit her on a wicker chair when the sun was at its highest point. I even made her a rattle out of little shells. I told her all kinds of stories and sang her many lullabies.

⁂

At the window a lilac lily
Sleep little one sweetly.

Clear as the stream,
I cherish your grin.
Sleep, sleep . . .

Red cherry, red cherry
Could make you marry
Stone removed by a magic fairy.
Sleep, sleep . . .
Sit down my little darling
We have many things for sharing
Though I can't lighten your worries,
I'll help you not to be weary.
Sleep, sleep . . .

Dringulu-drangulu the guitar,
txunkurrun-txunkurrun the tambourine,
txalopin-txaloka let's clap
Violins, flutes, and finger snaps.

⁂

She would quiet down for a brief moment, mesmerized by my voice, even smiling at times as she stretched her arm to touch my face. Nevertheless, she would soon begin wailing, completely unsettled. Little by little though as time went on, she began babbling and each word she pronounced became a gift for me: "*pupu, fu, lolo, ma, taka-taka . . .*"

She was about three and her name was Lainoa.

Lilia could not stand the rapport between the child and me: her sense of authority became eaten away by the worm of jealousy.

One afternoon the child drowned in the river.

I howled when she surfaced in the water.

"Be quiet. Quiet! You are wasting your time. Your crying won't bring 'your' child back," Lilia scolded me.

I dashed up to her and began to pull her hair and claw at her. We ended on the ground, exhausted, next to each other sighing.

"You devil, why did you kill the child?"

"She went to the river by herself. She inched down the dock steps on all fours, all the way to the water. She advanced calmly, like a little lady, saying "*apa-apa*" as if she knew where she was going. I let her go. Don't you know that wild animal mothers let their cubs die when they are seriously wounded?"

That very day, secretly, I stole a mare from the mill and left Lilia's house without saying goodbye. I tied the mare to the cart, placed my few belongings inside a chest, kept the seven pearls in my mind and lit a candle in the library. For once Lilia did not guess my thoughts. Is it hard to guess why?

When she realized I was gone, Lilia began calling my name in complete despair:

"My dearest Doltza, where have you gotten lost?"

I could hear her moaning from seven leagues away.

Each time I turned my head, I saw huge flames roaring where the mill was.

How do I dare? I left Lilia, the brave and generous, jealous and dignified, powerful and seductive Lilia Leakoa; the one who commanded, "Let it be done as I wish."

Yet, I could not put aside my hatred toward her and her insults followed me closely at all times.

"Thief! Liar! Coward! Weak! My eighth pearl!"

For a long time I felt my chest full of stinging nettle and pictured mountains as stone waves crashing on me. With no direction, I slept in ditches, ate insects, and stabbed my nails in my flesh, poisoned by the rabid foam of fury. I lived trapped in misery for a while. I was nothing but a personified wound, overwhelmed by pain.

Thankfully one night I dreamt of Lainoa, and felt such warmth in my dream that I woke up healed from all anger.

I dreamt that we both were little children, two children sitting on a pew of an old church. She no longer cried. The church was about to collapse and there were nuns waiting for us on one side, some wore white wimples and others black ones. Suddenly, Lainoa told me "Look after your children," and I said, "What children are you referring to?" And she replied, "Your words," and I said "Ah!" and she said" I must leave now. Give me a little kiss"; and the nuns came and took her, flying through the cracks of the colorful glass windows of the church.

Since then, every time I remember Lainoa, I think of the smell of warm milk or I discern the sound of shells.

As the water *plas-plas* falls from one blade to another once again to return, so does the past turn into the present, and the present into the future, to once again return the future to the past. The shaft of the mill rotates the stone, and the stone *txak, txak, txak*, grinds life while turning the grain into flour, shell into sand, flesh into dust, life into water . . .

And water into ice and fog, mud and waterfall, frost and ocean, hail and dew, still water and wave.

Because the path of water is the hieroglyph of life.

Mother Appeared to Doltza

Nikola remains asleep.

Doltza is awake and wearing a crown of flowers.

A woman is advancing toward her in the direction of the stream.

Doltza rubs her eyes, amazed at what she sees.

It's Mother, wearing a gown made of gray cloth. Her hair looks silver and, even though the rings under her eyes seem deeper, her eyes still look as lively as squirrels.

"Urria, my beloved daughter! What are you doing here?"

"I'm resting, Mother, I'm exhausted."

"Are you taking care of yourself?"

"Before, I could dance all night long but now a couple of dances are enough to wear me out."

"You used to be quick like a lizard, dear, but now you have turned into a donkey, a stout donkey. And as a donkey, all you do is work and work even if it's just with your voice. Thankfully, you don't bray. Haven't I ever told you? You were born on an autumn Sunday, on the seventh day of October, *Urria*, and that's how you got your name. I was laboring hard to bring you in to this world, overtaken by tension as the birthing took a turn for the worse: you were coming breeched. I think sometimes that's how you still live, backward . . . Oh well. The midwife first informed me that they would need to cut my stomach open with a saw and then, introduced a funnel into my mouth to pour booze down my throat. I got drunk at once. Nevertheless, it hurt! It was such an indescribable pain, the worst pain of pains, a maddening pain. The surgery, with the streams of blood and screams, resembled a pig slaughtering. But just when I was about to pass out, an angel appeared before me."

"Listen, Ana," the angel said, "under these circumstances two things might happen: You will either die and your child will lose her mother or you will deafen her with your screams. If the second happens, she will live a boring life for she will miss the sounds of this world." Though overwhelmed by pain, I argued with the angel until we came to an agreement. The angel would take a few years of my life in exchange for giving you a clear voice, sharp hearing, and quick eyes. And my beautiful child, you were born not only with those gifts but also with clear skin and a clean scent. Do not look at me with outrage. I know that you would have managed to live seven hours in this world without those gifts . . .

"What are you saying Mother? I didn't know that. Now I understand why destiny made me cross paths with that blind man when I found myself lacking faith and direction in life. Once my mare hurt its leg and . . ."

"What mare are you saying? You have a mare? Really?"

"A close friend gave it to me as a gift."

Doltza learned a long time ago how to partially disguise the truth without turning it into a lie.

And she continued:

"It was an excellent gift and I could hitch my cart to it. Because before, I had to pull the cart myself which almost made me grow a hump, like a camel. And that's not all. That friend also gave me seven pearls."

"Seven pearls? You must not be dumb."

"Seven pieces of advice. With those and my voice I have been able to make a living and . . . But we were talking about my mare, Mother. If you only knew how much I appreciate her. I go anywhere I want with her. I named her Haizelarrosa. We often ride at a gallop. Galloping is like being free."

"Galloping, trotting, or walking, the important thing is to move, to feel free," adds Mother.

"Once when we were on a rocky path, Haizelarrosa got hurt and began limping. I could not stand seeing her like that because what hurts her hurts me.

"And?"

Doltza begins telling her what happened:

"I entered a roadside inn looking for help. Sitting in a corner, downcast, was a blind man. When I walked by him, he lifted his head and began sniffing the air just as hunting dogs do for their masters. He said: "Oh, this blessed scent! This smell tells me that the one who just came in is in distress."

Because that man, though blind, could see through his sense of smell.

He perceived me through his nostrils and learned everything about me at once, as I am about to tell you. I hadn't said a word yet. I was four steps away from him and truly disturbed, I told him:

"My mare just hurt her leg."

"Take me to where the mare is," he ordered me.

We went to the stable and then, though a blind man, he saw the mare through his sense of hearing. He placed his ear against Haizelarrosa's chest, and though I am not sure what her heartbeats told him, after rubbing her legs, the mare's lips, up to then completely distorted from pain, relaxed and so did mine because I too had been in despair until then.

"When the thistle flower floats in the air, I feel it," the blind man told me.

I patted the mare, and shook the man's hand. He screamed: "Oh, this blessed skin! Let me read what your skin has to say."

He took my hand in his and followed the lifelines in my palm with his index finger, first forward, then back, stopping later while pressing his fingertips. He saw my past, present, and future along the paths of my hand. And while he was at it, he nodded his head, because that man, though blind, could see through his touch.

Then to show him how grateful I was, I asked him: "How can I pay you for what you have done for me?"

"Give me your voice," he replied.

I became frightened by his request: How could I grant him that ridiculous wish? I couldn't; "If I gave it to you, I would no longer be me. You don't want my voice, instead you want my words, because a voice is worth nothing without words."

"The same as having eyes with no images. You owe me a favor," he replied starting to get angry.

"But the same way images are created by one's own eyes, so does the voice need one's own words. Listen, we'll make another deal," I said. "I will tell you a few words that will only be for you, because no one will ever hear them except you and me at this very moment."

"And what kind of words did you tell him, my sweet daughter? The kind that hurt your ears or the other kind?"

"I told him something and the blind man's pupils gleamed, alert."

"Oh, this blessed voice! With every single word you have granted me a thousand images," he continued. "You are so fortunate for having the five senses and their gates placed where they belong. Two eyes to see and learn, two ears to listen and hear, a nose to smell and detect, a mouth to taste and speak, your skin to feel and make feel. And even if you are not aware of it, together with your sight, hearing, sense of smell, taste and touch, you have another, sixth sense, which happens to be an extension of the others. Balance. Balance to walk straight and get up when you fall—and after the sixth one, an additional one, a seventh one, an extraordinary sense!"

"I have an extraordinary sense and I haven't noticed it? It can't be," I said with a hint of suspicion.

"'Waterness' is the seventh one! The ability to mimic water. Oh, such a blessing to be able to behave like water. Those are your seven gifts, like seven white pieces of linen," and then he placed two kisses on my forehead. Suddenly, he shed two dry-leaf-like objects from his eyelids, and he began seeing, in a different way.

"As you see, Mother, I paid my debt with words though I'm not sure if it was because of the melody of the words or because of the blind's man's faith. Mother, as you might understand, I can't repeat those words in your presence, because they were special and unique, as we are. Even if I tried, it would be in vain because it would require a long time to do so, at least one hour less than eight, at the very least . . .

"Oh my! What a beautiful crown you are wearing!" The mother interrupts the daughter's babbling without trying to be mean but with no patience.

"Nikola Brinkola made it for me. No one has given me anything like this in a long time."

Nikola, still asleep, rolls over on the grass.

"But aren't those wild roses? My dear, they are full of thorns. Don't you know that there are no roses without thorns? Take it off at once, silly girl."

The mother stretches her arm to take off Doltza's crown.

"No, no, don't. It's mine. I want it!"

The mother takes the crown off her daughter's forehead abruptly.

"I bet you don't ask for it three times before the cock crows."

ANA URKIZA

Ondarroa, 1969

*A*na Urkiza holds a bachelor's degree in information sciences and is an expert in business communication. She mostly writes short stories and has won the Agustin Zubikarai and Tene Mujika prizes, among many others.

Some of the books she has published include the short story collections, *Desira Izoztuak* (Frozen desires, 2002) *Bekatuak* (Sins, 2005), *Atzorako geratzen dena* (aforismoak), (What is left for yesterday [aphorisms], 2011); the poetry volumes, *Gela ilunetik* (From the dark room, 2000), *Bazterreko ahotsa* (The background voice, 2002); children's and young adult books, *Betaurrekoak ditut eta zer?* (I wear glasses, so? 2001*)*, *Hondartzako kioskoa* (The newsstand at the beach, 2001), *Ondarruko piratak* (The pirates from Ondarrua, 2003), *Amak plastakoa eman dit* (Mom slapped me, 2004), *Nire herriak ostadarraren koloreak ditu* (My town is the color of the rainbow, 2006), and *Nire hiriko poemak* (Poems from my city, 2006); *Bidegorriko festa* (Trail Fest, 2010); *Sekretuaren zaporea* (The flavor of the secret, 2011); *Azazkalak jaten ditut, eta zer?*, (I bite my fingernails, so?, 2012); *Zortzi unibertso, zortzi idazle*, (Eight universes, eight writers, 2006); *Augustin Zubikarai (biografia)*, (Agusting Zubikarai, 2008); and Atzorako geratzen dena (aforismoak), (What is left for yesterday [aphorisms], 2011).

Faraway Ties

*H*ow should she break the news to Marco? Silvia anguished over it. She felt completely lost for words, betrayed, and as ugly as always. Although she remembered that Marco assured her to the contrary, she was convinced now, more than ever, of the connection between misfortune and lack of beauty.

As she recalled Marco's words, she thought of Rome, the day they met in Rome. That sunny day in April, she and Zezilia were at the Fontana Di Trevi enjoying the beauty of the art that surrounded them and admitting that the last five months of planning had been worth it.

Although those were not memories from long ago, they could dissipate easily, at any time.

"Don't look," Zezilia told her, elbowing her in the side, but those guys who just sat on the left are staring at us!"

"They must be looking at you, pretty thing!" thought Silvia. Based on experience, she knew that whenever she was with Zezilia, guys never showed any interest in her.

But overtaken by curiosity, furtively, she cast a brief look in their direction and met the sweet smile of a stranger.

"You're right!" she told Zezilia nervously, thrilled. "They are looking at us."

The one who shared the first smile walked up to Zezilia and told her in Italian; *"Io sono Carlo,"* mimicking selected words out of a tourist guide. Zezilia began to converse with Carlo in a kind of pseudo-Italian. When he realized that Zezilia did not understand part of what he was saying, he told them that he was with a friend and invited them to go meet him. When the girls did not move, he yelled *"Marco,"* calling his friend sitting a few steps away as he motioned his arms so he would join them.

Silvia thought that Marco looked amazingly handsome, more so than Carlo. He had a darker complexion and green eyes; he was well dressed. Men like him did not even dare appear in her dreams.

As unbelievable as it seemed, Marco sat next to Silvia. When he asked her if she spoke English or French, Silvia replied that she did better in French.

Marco told her that he worked as a tour-guide, an interpreter and a translator as if to let her know that Italian men had something else between their ears besides thoughts of sex. Once they finished with introductory formality, they asked Silvia and Zezilia about the places they were planning to visit in Rome. The girls named the most famous landmarks and monuments in the city. The guys, on the other hand, suggested they should visit places not listed in typical tourist guides.

As night fell, they accompanied the girls to the San Pedro plaza where they were to catch their bus. They made a date to meet the next day.

The following day, they headed to the riverbank. Silvia, obeying an unfamiliar impulse, wore a short skirt that she had borrowed from a friend, washed her hair and let it down. Even before Marco told her she looked beautiful, she felt ready to be desired for the first time. And right there, by the river, with a piece of the Italian sky as a witness, as her Catholic grandmother would put it, "she lost her shame."

In a charming, loving gesture, Marco handed Silvia his telephone number to reassure her that what had just happened between them was not meaningless, that he was interested in her.

Silvia wondered if the thread they wound between them by having sex would end up being a fragile and hurtful one. She doubted that giving her his telephone number had been a good idea because it opened the door to hope when she knew that actually, in a few hours, they would leave Rome and would never see each other again. Nevertheless, she held the number tightly in her hand while, to her own surprise, she sighed and wished deeply (and secretly) to herself that what Marco was proposing turned out to be true.

When their remaining two days in Rome came to an end and they had to say their goodbyes, they met with Carlo and Zezilia. From his pocket, Carlo took out a coin punctured with a small hole and asked the girls for their phone numbers. He told them that they would keep their relationships alive by using the coin, his tool to make free calls from public phones, now dangling from a thread around his neck. The four of them burst into laughter, a nervous sounding laughter provoked by the tiniest ray of hope when faced with sadness. And as those who plant a seed look up to the sky hoping for rain, the young women felt a spark of hope inside them. The young men promised that if they made it through the winter, they would visit in summer. The girls believed them.

"I've never trusted one-day love affairs, much less feelings solely based on sex but I feel as if Marco were wrapped around my being," she told Zezilia when they left Rome.

When the trip was over and they returned home, Carlo and Marco began calling them every day at approximately nine in the evening, without fail. They called Zezilia's house first because the coin with the hole belonged to Carlo, the coin that the public phones never learned how to swallow; then they called Silvia.

Their mothers became accustomed to answering the phone in Italian

"Io sono mama de Zezilia" and *"Io sono mama de Silvia."* They loved hearing the lively inflection of the Italian language and partaking in their daughters' excitement.

And every day, Marco promised Silvia he would visit her in the summer, followed by an *"a demain."*

≈ ❦ ≈

But how was she supposed to give him the news in French? The question overtook her mind.

She knew that words can take on different meanings when not said or heard in one's own language. They often sound bigger and more serious than they really are. She also knew that the lack of understanding in a language offers the perfect excuse to ignore responsibilities. She knew that distance completely softens the intensity of responsibility and love and that it makes everything forgivable and understandable. She knew that if she told him the truth, she would put his summer visit at risk but, on the other hand, she couldn't keep the news from Marco; she could not tell him everything was fine. With the hope that love ignites and holds, that day, she got the strength to tell him the truth, in Italian.

"Marco, como sois?"

"Je suis bien, et tois?"

". . ."

Marco, like always, spoke to her in French, but Silvia tried her best to speak in Italian.

"Marco, well, I need to tell you something."

"Qu'est-ce que tu dis? Je ne comprends rien!"

"Well, I . . . recordare la noite de . . ."

"Mais, qu'est-ce que tu dis? Qu'est-ce que c'est la noite?"

". . ."

It was truly difficult to talk on the phone. Besides, Silvia was nervous. She needed time to get the right inflection, to get into the subject matter . . . But all Marco was expecting from Silvia was a sweet, easy conversation with a few *ha-has* here and there.

"Marco . . . Io bonbino tui, Marco!" she burst out finally, without beating about the bush.

". . ."

Silvia realized that the sentence she tried to convey in Italian did not make much sense but it was not that far off. She felt frustrated.

The other side of the line went silent. Marco knew he had to answer, that Silvia was waiting for an answer from his side.

Silvia thought that maybe, just maybe, she should have asked Zezilia for help, although she was not sure what for, to help her with the translation or to ask her for the strength she was lacking.

"Qu'est –ce que tu dis, ma chérie?" asked Marco again from the other side of the line.

Realizing that he was telling her that he did not understand what she said, she blurted, "Merde!" Now is too late to think of Zezilia.

"Merde? Qu'est ce-que tu as, ma chérie?"

She decided to continue in French.

"Rien, Marco . . . j'ai quelque chose á dire . . ." she meant to begin tenderly. Je suis desolé . . ."

". . ."

"Marco, je suis enceinte!"

". . ."

Silvia wanted to keep explaining, hoping to shorten distances, looking for support, wishing for some kind of reaction, imagining Marco's face . . .

But instead of all that, she heard the shameless, *tut-tut-tut* of the receiver.

As result of the weight of the news she passed on through the line, apparently, this time, the public phone swallowed the punctured coin . . .

Making a Boy

You told us about your job . . . incessantly . . . You made it clear that you are the breadwinner in your home. You forgot to clarify, though, that you work because your husband does not move a finger but, oh well . . . You did not complain at all about it but it was obvious that you two lived separate lives . . . During the week, due to your schedules, you hardly see each other. On Saturday afternoons you go to visit your mother and he goes to the bar to play cards. On Sundays, you go out with your daughter and your husband stays home watching cable.

You made it clear that you live a happy life . . . that you don't lack anything at home, that you have a beautiful daughter, a job that you like, a big house . . . and most importantly, that you are the sole owner of everything you do and all you have.

You don't mind if all days are the same. You let us know that you are accustomed to routine; that your daughter is not a baby any more and that you have begun, once again, enjoying your own life. You emphasized that you are not looking for any more complications; that you do not want more children because your daughter is all you need to feel fulfilled.

It took a lot out of you to say those last words because

many have told you that you should have more children and because you know that those who are even busier than you try to have a second child. You must have felt like you needed to justify yourself when you told us how much your daughter fulfills you.

You made it clear that your husband does not help you; that you do not share any common goals.

Nothing else need be said. We all understood what went unsaid.

All of us have thought or felt something similar, and all have fallen silent.

⚬ ❦ ⚬

You told us that you did not feel well. We offered you some water. But you preferred to leave because you were tired, and you asked your husband to take you home.

He stood up from his seat unwillingly.

"Women's things . . ." he said while feeling for the car keys in his pocket, grabbing his sweater from the back of the chair and putting it on his shoulders. "I better treat her tenderly . . . we are trying to make a boy . . . you know."

Our eyes pierced yours, seeking an explanation. Your face transformed.

"No kidding?" said one the friends to your husband. "I wouldn't be so cocky about it, buddy."

"It's a sure thing!" said your husband not ready to retreat. "A doctor has assured us that it has been scientifically proven."

"Just in case . . ." said the friend again.

Your eyes were downcast, you dared not breathe. Your husband missed your body language and kept at it.

"I bet our next one will be a boy!"

He boasted. You remained silent; avoided looking at anyone and did not even answer your husband. The presence of your menstruation provoked an expression on your face, which rendered all explanations unnecessary.

A New Cinderella

*D*olores felt overjoyed when, after becoming a widow, her daughter invited her to live with her.

But, she ended up doing all the cleaning, the cooking, the shopping, the ironing, the babysitting . . . She ended up doing it all.

When, after becoming a widow, her daughter invited her to live with her, she lost any hope of wearing the glass slippers and attending the ball.

ARANTXA ITURBE
Alegia, 1964

I am also a mother. That "also" still gives me more headaches than I want. Still and forever already.

I love my work at the radio station. I love listening and interviewing people. I love my job. I was a radio announcer before a mother.

And later I wrote, more than I do now. I always thought I wrote to tell stories but now I am not so sure. I am not really sure why I write. But I loved writing too. By writing I could give life to characters that said what I wanted to hear. I used to write before I was also a mother.

I once wrote about motherhood. From within. Without forgetting I was a mother but keeping in mind that being a mother was not a state of being. I did not write to give life to a character that would say what I wanted, instead, I wrote listening to what I said.

I did not recall if there were traces of mothers in stories. There are. Of some women that *were* before they ever were mothers. I abandoned them when I became a mother. I do not remember why.

I Bet She Has Curly Hair!

*E*very time we met for coffee at that hour of the day, she would arrive fifteen minutes late, out of breath, place her purse on the chair and say; "Let me tell you, it's impossible to find a parking space in this town, my friend." And take off her jacket and say; "I'm drenched in sweat" then, take a seat and say; "I'm exhausted."

That day, she arrived fifteen minutes late, out of breath, and placed her purse on the chair and said; "let me tell you, it's impossible to find a parking space in this town, my friend." And took off her jacket and said; "I'm drenched in sweat" then took her seat and said; "I'm pregnant."

She only changed one word. Otherwise, she ordered her usual: coffee, very dark and as Imanol placed the cup before her, she lit her first cigarette.

I must have not understood correctly. "If she were pregnant, she wouldn't smoke," I thought and calmed down.

She must've read my dumbfounded face.

"I'll quit," she said, sounding like she found it hard to believe her own words. "Gradually. I cannot change my habits from one day to the next. How are you?"

"Well, I'm surprised. How do you expect me to be after hearing such news?" It had been about two months since we last had seen each other. How long had she known about it?

"I found out a month ago." And not a call, no nothing? Did the father know?

She said no one knew yet. I asked what she was going to do.

"Do?" she asked. "The doing part is done. Now, all that's left to do is wait for seven months. That's all!"

I would not be as surprised if, instead of Paola, it had been Maribel. When we used to smoke our first clandestine cigarettes in the restroom, Maribel was sure she would never smoke because she wanted to have children before too long. When we wrote the names of our first boyfriends on the corners of our papers and then crumble them and throw them to each other during religion class, she would frown at us because she thought it was shameful to change the names daily. She only loved one; we all knew who. We all knew that it was useless for her to love him, who only had room for soccer in his head. But Maribel was convinced that he was going to be her children's father.

When we, so proud of ourselves, started sharing stories about our first experiences, she told us that we would come to regret it some day.

When we had the opportunity to go away to college, Maribel, not wanting to be far from the one-on-the-path-to-soccer-stardom, preferred to stay home.

The one-on-the-path-to-soccer-stardom, got stuck on the path when, during a soccer clinic which was crucial for his future, became infatuated with a girl; infatuated with a girl that he got pregnant. He got her pregnant and they were forced to get married. We tried to cheer Maribel up. At least, from then on she would think of something else besides soccer and we hoped that she would turn into a more normal person. Of course, it is a tremendous blow in life to lose the father of your imaginary children, especially for someone who lived without room to dream other dreams.

We felt heartbroken when she came up to us crying, asking what she should do with the little pink sweaters and onesies she kept in her attic. "The one who's going to have his child will be able to make good use of them," said Paola. As she stood there in complete silence in front of us, her nose running, we realized that this was not a joking matter for Maribel. And the situation would only get worse as time went on.

Later, we learned from others—she never communicated with us—that she began acting as if she had lost her mind. She would approach anyone she saw pushing a baby stroller and ask them when the baby had been born, how much she weighed, if she cried a lot, how often she had to be fed and if she had to be held up right to be burped.

By the time the one-on-the-path-to-soccer-stardom began having arguments with his wife in public, Maribel had found a new hero for her dreams. Luis. Luis was the youngest of eight, he believed that the home of an only child was very sad, and he was an electrician. Those had been the first words Maribel told me when we bumped into each other after our university years.

I replied that I was thrilled for her.

* ✿ *

"It's a matter of statistics," Paola continued, talking and smoking.

"Pure statistics. One out of a hundred. My luck."

I asked her to leave statistics for other matters. For percentages of those who terminate their pregnancies, for example.

She looked at me as if I had lost my mind.

"You tell me that, knowing that I'm the one percent?"

◆ ❦ ◆

All her new friends think of the same gift for Paola: a watch, because they do not realize, until they know her a little better, that she can't tell time. In nights with a full moon, Paola loves to step out to the balcony to sing. She is liable to start a letter, get bored and send it without having finished writing it. Every year, I receive a Christmas card from her telling me how much she hates Christmas cards. She never ends up going on vacation where she planned to go. Most travel agencies would know who you were talking about if you mentioned the woman who, at the very last minute, changes her ticket to go to one corner of the world for a ticket for the opposite corner. A job has never lasted longer than six months. Once, a boyfriend outlasted her job, and two days later she called him to let him know that she got fired and that it would be better if they stopped seeing each other. (Even today, the poor guy still doesn't understand what he did to get Paola fired. "I hardly called her at work because I didn't want to bother her," he tells me every time I see him.) She can call you at three in the morning to let you know that she is moving to Canada, and a week later she might be oblivious to what she told you. Another time she confided in me that she was ready to leave every thing behind to begin a new life in India with a Swedish waiter she met at a Chinese restaurant. On her way to the train station, she fell in love with a wonderful taxi driver from Astigarraga; her trip ended two kilometers from her home and right there she began her new life that lasted a total of three months.

What's worse is that she forgets everything. Sometimes, when she must make life and death decisions and I remind her about her latest decision, she opens her eyes wide and gazes at me in wonder. "You have such a good memory," she says, "and then what?" she asks. And that is when I tell her the rest of the story and she listens to me attentively as if I were telling her a story about an old friend. Sometimes, when I finish, all that's left for her is to break into applause.

⁂

"This is not a tale, Paola, this is your life. Yours and someone else's now," I say somberly because such is the situation.

"I bet she has curly hair!"

"Is this a matter of statistics too?"

"No, my friend, don't mix concepts! This is a matter of probability! It's going to have curly hair."

We got very busy during the following months, looking for everything she was going to need. Once in a while, just in case, I reminded her that her new life did not have a point of return.

"Don't pester me," she told me.

If any acquaintance asked her if she was having a boy or a girl, she replied, "curly hair."

"Aren't they a pain?" she would say genuinely, while smiling at me.

She never told me anything about the one with curly hair and I never asked her either. But as the due date was getting closer, I could not keep quiet any longer.

"Aren't you going to say anything to 'curly'?"

Paola was not one to hide things, yet it seemed that she had been trying to ignore the matter for months and I thought it was time to do something about it.

Paola did not agree with me.

"I didn't expect that from you," she said.

That was all.

৶ ❦ ৶

When the moment came, she did not call me even though we had agreed she would. The neighbor that accompanied her called to let me know that she had given birth to a daughter and that both mother and baby were doing well.

I went to visit her and brought her some mint truffles. She looked tired and welcomed me with a bittersweet smile. When I got close to the baby, she said:

"Probabilities failed me. Look at her!"

She did not give me enough time.

"Thankfully, I didn't say anything to 'Curly'!" And she burst into laughter. An uncontrollable stream of laughter.

I sat on the bed and embraced her to ease the path of Paola's laughter into tears.

Two Pimples

The same day I fell in love I became pregnant. A huge blunder. Two blunders, to be more exact. One right after the other and in that order. But I didn't become pregnant because of a blunder. I got pregnant on purpose. And I didn't fall in love because of a blunder. But I didn't fall in love on purpose the same day.

Nevertheless, both didn't happen simultaneously. First, I fell in love. And then, I became pregnant. For a couple months after the blunders happened I didn't know how to fix the problem. To be more concise, I didn't know how to fix my two problems. On one hand, I didn't know how to tell the father-to-be that I had fallen in love with the one who wasn't going to be the father, and on the other hand, I didn't know how to tell the one who wasn't going to be a father that I was going to be a mother.

I chose the easiest way. I didn't tell either one anything.

I ended up with two pimples, one on each cheek.

One worried me a lot, the other one not at all. It was just one more pimple.

Pimples and I share a long history. My friends have often laughed at me because of my pimples. It's not a laughing matter but my pimples have always been funny. Most likely because they haven't been the kind to suffer over, as far as pimples and suffering go.

They have always sprouted individually. Huge, noticeable, drawing attention, but always individually. By the time one disappeared, the second one would be popping out and at the most inconvenient times, before the first two disappeared, the third one would be on its way to breaking ground. Never more than that. And sometimes I didn't get any.

I always feared them, probably because, since I was a child, my mother frequently talked to me about pimples. In my childhood, she never allowed me to eat chocolate because she feared I would get pimples. But obviously my attraction to chocolate was stronger than my fear of pimples, considering how much chocolate I ate, that is until I got a little older, and even though I did not have any pimples then, I began eating chocolate more moderately. That is when I solved the mystery of pimples: Whenever I ate tons of chocolate, I never got a single pimple, unlike when I began eating less. Coincidentally, it happened to be about the time when my peers stopped getting them.

When I stumbled upon my first pimple, I cursed all the chocolate in the world. Blinded by fury, I didn't realize that I hadn't had any chocolate for the last week. But unquestionably, that bump protruding in the middle of my right cheek had to be the result of the many kilos of chocolate I had consumed in all those previous years. That was the only reason I could come up with.

All I could think of, to stem my anger was to eat chocolate. And that is exactly what I did until I grew bored and yet, no more pus craters protruded. The one already on my cheek went through its life cycle by growing, growing, growing, and when it looked like it was ready to erupt, by becoming smaller, smaller, smaller, until it disappeared. Gone.

Although it might seem unreal how time-consuming it can be to think about pimples, I spent hour after hour thinking of my very first pimple. I kept looking for a logical explanation but, since I connected the pimple with eating chocolate, I couldn't find one. At least in my case, I didn't believe that eating chocolate was the root of my pimples.

I decided to conduct a test. I quit eating chocolate. The first day nothing happened. The second day, I almost ate a piece but I toughed it out and didn't have it. The third day, I woke up with the urge to eat chocolate. Together with my urge came the pimple that confirmed my theory: my body needed chocolate to stay clean of pimples.

From then on, untroubled, I went back to eating chocolate.

One morning when I woke up with a red nose, I came to the realization that eating chocolate and my pimples were not directly connected. The reason for my pimples was wanting something. When I was obsessed with chocolate, it was chocolate. But when I began obsessing about other things, it was other things.

It is extremely difficult to tell someone "You've been a pimple in my life." That is precisely why I haven't said that to anyone although more than once, I've found myself on the verge of doing so.

I told my friends. I told my friends my theory and that was my undoing. Every time they would see a new pimple on my cheek, they knew that I was infatuated with something new.

"A new craving?" they asked me, looking at a pimple that I could not disguise.

I often regretted having told them anything. I tried many

times to convince them that, my pimples are due to stress as my esthetician tells me. But they have proof to the contrary unlike my esthetician who is convinced it is all due to nerves. I'm sure of it too. A special nervousness that emerges while I wait to obtain something. I've never had a date without pimples. I should clarify. The dates I've had with no pimples have ended up just as that, mere dates. Dates that I've had with pimples (counting the pimple, three of us) have never been one-time dates. In those cases at least two more dates followed.

The day I had a lunch-date with Koldo, I had one of the biggest pimples I've ever had on my left cheek. I didn't touch it. That's usually best, to leave it alone so it follows its course. I knew, or I thought I knew, who provoked it. I had been dreaming for some time now of being alone with him. And at last, though not as soon as I hoped, the occasion arrived. The pimple had surfaced a few days earlier to confirm the increasing strength of the craving. I thought that this time it surfaced earlier than on other occasions because it was taking me longer to get what I wanted (until then, the blemishes surfaced the very same day of the date.) I didn't worry when, before lunch, while in the restroom I noticed a second one popping out on my right cheek. I just thought that the craving was very strong this time.

By dessert I had fallen in love. We stayed together until dark, coming up with all kinds of excuses not to part. We both knew we had to return to our respective homes. We said our goodbyes promising to meet again and I went home as late as ever.

My husband was waiting for me. He didn't seem surprised at my late arrival. He had his plans all made. We had been talking for a long time, half seriously, half jokingly, about having a baby and he told me that the time was right to make a baby. That's what he told me. And with no time for me to come up with an excuse, he began to undress.

"Not just one but two!" he said all of a sudden.

I wasn't sure what he was talking about. Apparently he had discovered my second pimple. And he might've reached the conclusion: "This means that you are eager to have a baby."

No sooner said than done.

I, in the mean time, laughed to myself, what a fool, he thought that the pimples betrayed me, he lived believing that he knew all about me. He recognized the symptoms but only I knew their true interpretation. From the day we met, pimples and all, of course, I had to come up with many stories to hide the real reasons that explained the presence of my pimples.

Now I'm pregnant and in love and with two pimples. I'm afraid that this time I might have gone too far.

I don't worry about Koldo. I've had many pimples in my life. They go as they come, once they have completed their course. As the craving turns into love and love turns into nothingness, so does a pimple surface with a craving and disappear when the craving has passed. But if the first pimple is, as I suspect, a reflection of wanting a baby, I'm doomed. This means that it will stay with me for seven more months. And I'm not sure what will happen when the baby is born. Perhaps I won't get any more pimples. And I might feel sorry for people with pimples as I think of all the unfulfilled cravings they might harbor.

JASONE OSORO IGARTUA

Elgoibar, 1971

Jasone Osoro Igartua holds a degree in information science and has completed graduate studies in screenplay writing. As a journalist she has worked in the print media as well as in television as a scriptwriter.

She has published two collections of short stories *Tentazioak* (Temptations, 1998) and *Korapiloak* (Knots, 2001.) In children's, and young adult's literature, she has published *Jara* (Jara, 2001), *Jara, bikiak eta bikoteak* (Jara, twins and couples, 2005), *Jara Bartzelonan* (Jara in Barcelona, 2007), and *Ezekiel* (Ezekiel, 2009) *Jara live* (2010), *Ezekiel nora ezean* (Ezekial adrift, 2012) *Muma mamua* (Muma the ghost, 2014). She is also the author of a biography of Isadora Duncan. She has published a novel, *Greta* (2003) in which motherhood is the main theme. She has also published an essay, which could be considered autobiographical *Bi marra arrosa* (Two pink lines, 2009).

These last two works present very different views on motherhood. *Greta* is about abandonment, unwanted pregnancy, and its consequences. *Bi marra rosa* is about the opposite, desired, enjoyed, and planned pregnancy. The story we have selected for this anthology lies between those two. It suggests a love story, a new relationship between a mother and a son. It's about a moment that endures with absence and abandonment, but reads very differently. "Love Is a Puzzle" is about new types of motherhood.

Love Is a Puzzle

The day I turned nine my mother handed me a present, a tape recorder and then she disappeared from my life. Once a year I received a cassette tape where pieces of my mother's life had been recorded, and gradually, only the image of the mole she had on her cheek and the name Laura, which belonged to the woman whose voice made me fall in love, survived in my memory.

I was twenty-five years old when I rented a flat downtown, which I shared with Daniela and her grandmother, Teresa. And it was then when on a foggy morning, unexpectedly, I found my mother's last tape placed by the front door. The deep, thick voice that only I knew revealed her face, and that same day I fell even more in love with the image I had come to idealize.

That weekend, in an effort to recover lost time, we spent almost every minute of the forty eight-hours together. She bought me lollypops as if I were a child and I held her hand every time the traffic light changed, as a frightened son would do. I loved Mother's smell: the smell of the tobacco she smoked, blended with the Heno de Pravia soap scent that covered her skin. At night, in bed, I fell asleep after resting my cheek on the scarf that I had secretly stolen from her.

"Good morning Karlos. It looks like the perfect day to go to the beach. I'm going to wax my legs while you have breakfast. I saw that your roommate has some wax in the bathroom. She won't mind if I use it, will she?"

"No, I don't think Daniela will mind."

While I dunked a muffin in milk, Mother warmed up the wax. As I took a bite of the muffin, I almost choked when I saw Mother, right there, in the middle of the kitchen before my eyes, taking off her skirt and sitting on a chair ready to wax her legs. As I recalled, that was the first time I saw my mother's thighs. They looked a bit fatter and shorter than I had dreamt, but Mother's real thighs were much more beautiful and perfect than I had imagined. She had meaty knees and fine ankles, and her feet were as small and playful as those of a child.

"How's the city, dear?"

She was always the one asking the questions. I was speechless. Through all those years while she sent me the tapes, I thought of a thousand questions, but now, when I had Mother in front of me, I felt like a teenager in front of the girl he likes, flustered, foolish, embarrassed.

"Good. Daniela and Teresa are wonderful and I enjoy living with them."

"And, you don't have a girlfriend?"

"No, no!!!"

Mother rolled a bit of hot wax around some kind of a wooden stick and spread it on, from top to bottom. First on her left leg and then on her right. She rested the stick on the jar, lifted a tip of the hardened wax and, *zast!* She pulled a section. I felt pain but Mother's face did not change its expression and she repeated it on her other leg. The hair that had covered Mother's skin was now stuck onto the wax. Watching Mother wax had a calming effect on me. The eucalyptus scent of the green-colored wax wafted through the kitchen and dazed me. I kept dunking the muffins and devouring them nonstop, as lovers with only one night left to be together tirelessly keep kissing. I wish I could have been the wooden stick. I wanted to take the hot, liquid wax in my mouth and get stuck on Mother's body. But it hurt me to think of the moment when the heat would turn into cold and the liquid into solid because I knew that would be the moment to pull on the wax. I knew that I would never smell Mother's warm sweat, or touch it, and I knew also that we would need to go our separate ways soon. When she was about to pull the wax covering her knee area, she blurted:

"I'm getting married."

These words pierced my ears as if they were nails. My eyes filled with heavy, leaden tears carried through veins, turbid rivers.

"To whom?"

I had to know. I needed to know who the man was who would steal my mother from me a second time.

"You don't know him, darling."

"But, how? When? Why?"

So many questions darted through my mind, one after another. All the unknowns hurt my mouth in the same way alcohol both burns and heals a wound but I had to ask them.

"Next Saturday, my darling."

". . ."

"I don't want to live alone, darling."

She finished waxing and I closed the muffin bag. I came up to Mother, took the wooden stick from her hand and began rolling the wax on and on.

"Will you still send me recordings?" I asked her.

"Yearly, like I have until now."

"Will you let me wax your upper thighs?"

I'm not sure why I asked her such a thing. Perhaps, because I thought that would be the last opportunity I had to touch her skin. Perhaps, because that was the only way to pull out the nails piercing my heart.

"Have you ever done it?"

"No, never."

"Will you know how to?"

"..."

I piled wax on the wooden stick and spread it on Mother's thigh from side to side. I felt a unique sensation, odd. For a moment I imagined I was a snake licking Mother's entire body with my tongue, as if I wanted to poison her, bewilder her, drive her mad, and keep her in my imaginary world, make her mine.

"Now you must rest the stick on the jar and pull the wax with your hand," she said.

It was difficult; it hurt me to have to peel off my own poison. But Mother held my hand, and together we pulled, zast!

"You have your father's hands. Big. Your father's hands were big and black. They were always dirty when he came home from the factory and the black machine oil could never be cleaned from under his nails, not with soap, bleach, or ammonia. But I loved your father's hands because they were big and black.

She hardly spoke about Father and it surprised me to hear her talk about his hands the very same day she told me she was about to get married.

"Why are you getting married, Mother?"

"Do you see those billboards outside?" When she opened the window, I felt as if the south wind had brought a cold front. "They are off during the day and turn into a party at night, all dressed up in lights. They are nothing but artificial signs of happiness. As if owning a television set, shoes, a car, or a cell phone would make everything right. They want to make us believe that by drinking a martini, a handsome guy wearing sunglasses will be attracted to us. Life is not that easy."

"But those ads show us pieces of reality."

"You said it, pieces. That's precisely why I'm getting married, darling, because my heart is made up of pieces and because, in order to keep it whole, I need all the pieces to fit.

"A heart is not a puzzle."

"But love is. Love is a puzzle."

Right there, facing the billboards where ads were dressed up in sequence, I took the woman standing in front of me in my arms and kissed her on the mouth. She did not say or do anything. She looked me in the eye, took my big hand and placed it on her breast, on the left one. On her heart.

"Do you feel the pieces? And your piece?" she asked me. I didn't answer her; I wanted to become one with the skin of the breast I was cupping.

"Will you let me wax your legs?"

Each time I peeled off a piece of wax, a scream that bubbled up inside me would silently burst.

A week later a biker my age married my mother. My private Marylin.

GARAZI KAMIO ANDUAGA

Andoain, 1979

*G*arazi Kamio Anduaga holds degrees in audio-visual communication and education. She has worked in media, including the Basque Television literature program *Sautrela*. Garazi's first published work is the short story collection, *Beste norbaiten Zapatak* (Someone else's shoes, 2012), where gender occupies a prominent role. She has written two stories touching on motherhood, "325" and "Panenka" which has been chosen for this collection.

Panenka

With gravity at work, you witnessed each centimeter of the fall. Your mother's Bohemian crystal vase shattered into a thousand pieces and the sentence she uttered next echoed in your head: "Don't worry, I didn't like it that much anyway." Her words sounded to you like a lie as fat as your daughter's soccer ball. The blow of the crystal vase knocked you right on the head once again shaking your convictions. You are not sure what kind of a cynical face you made at that moment. She has always liked the vase; it's her most beloved decoration in the whole house. When you were a child she went on-and-on about how your father brought it for her from faraway Bohemia; that it was a one-of-a-kind hand-made vase and that he had to smuggle it in so the customs police would not confiscate it.

He brought the crystal vase to Mother from a trip to Czechoslovakia, the only trip your father ever made abroad. There was also a special tray in your house. Until Irati hit it with her soccer ball and it dropped to the floor, that is. The tray also broke in front of Mother's and your eyes. On that occasion, once again, you felt embarrassed. You imagined the sonar of a ship, searching for the worst mother ever. Yesterday you pictured the sonar once again. And again you were the green target it identified.

Your mother and you wrapped the Bohemian crystal vase in newspaper and threw it in the trash. You felt that all those childhood days of years past ended up wrapped inside the papers. When you were a child, they forbade you to play in the living room. With the arrival of Irati, the new generation, the ban on living room play was lifted and now the new generation has just shattered the very object of the original prohibition.

They have always allowed Irati to do as she pleases in the living room. You reminded her many times that playing soccer in her grandparents' home is not allowed; that the living room is for watching TV or reading. That is what they taught you. Now, however, they grant their granddaughter all kinds of privileges and freedom. Mother tells her one thing and Grandmother tells her another. While you stick to the mother role given to you in this play, Grandmother goes off the script.

At the end, as usual, you lose. And your bedmate thought the vase incident was, like many other issues in life, a trifle.

You chose Martin because you hated soccer. He was not the trimmest or the nicest guy in your group of friends but he was the only one who happened to dislike soccer and you knew for sure that you were not going to marry a hooligan like your father. There was no room for a soccer ball in your dream-life, until your daughter's obsession awakened you.

While you were pregnant, all you hoped for was a boy. Your father hoped for an heir that would share his passion for soccer. You, on the other hand, hoped for the brother that you kept asking of your mother for when you were a child. As soon as you got married, you began following useless superstitions like eating the heel of the loaf of bread in order to give birth to a boy. Wasted effort: you had a girl. And still, when you see Irati wearing the Betis jersey, you feel a piercing pain in your heart: "have I created a second division daughter?"

Sometimes the passion she feels for Betis mortifies you. There are those in town who like Barcelona and Real Madrid. "At least if she were a Barcelona fan . . ." Thankfully, she doesn't like Real Madrid. If she did, more than one person would hate her. You are not sure why Irati likes Betis. There are no famous players on their roster nor do they run great advertising campaigns. But all your daughter thinks about is soccer and Betis.

More than once you have been tempted to throw her green and white striped jersey away. You still believe that soccer is a boys' sport and you have repeated it to her time and again. You often think that you are old-fashioned. Your father bought her the complete Betis uniform. It doesn't really make a difference to him if she likes Betis, Real, or Alcoyano, as long as she likes soccer. You, on the other hand, have told him frequently that he should not mention soccer to her. You think it is better to buy her books and games as presents. Your dad and you do not see eye-to-eye on this and have often fought about it.

Your husband tells you that you do things in a rush. Apparently, one should stop and think twice before acting because decisions made without thinking result in problems. Martin is too laidback; it takes him too long to make a decision. Two opposites, from the day you met. The only thing you two had in common was how much you both hated soccer. Another subtle argument to prove that you make decisions too quickly.

Today your father and you went to pick her up from school. As you were waiting for the traffic light to change, you saw about thirty skaters on the pathway. You also used to skate when you were a child. "In your day, you kids were not as skilled," Father told you. You aimed a sharp look in his direction. You were a pretty good skater in your childhood. Father never saw you: soccer and work kept him busy most of the day. When you were at home, Mother always asked you to take the skates off. That Bohemia crystal vase caused you so much pain . . .

You see schoolchildren running. Your eyes search for Irati. You find her; she's coming your way running too. She hands you the Betis backpack Grandfather gave her and kisses you both.

They begin talking about soccer. Xabi Alonso this, Xabi Alonso that, says your father. He hates Real Madrid with all his might. He considers this player a traitor. Apparently, it is not right to wear the Real Madrid jersey if one is Basque. You, on the other hand, couldn't care less if Xabi Alonso wears a white jersey or not. You think that your father has influenced Irati. The other day, as she was watching the sports, you heard her say "Guti, faggot." You punished her with no TV, but once again, Martin, the peacemaking mediator, worked you to go easy on her.

Next week, Betis is coming to Anoeta to play and Father has bought two tickets to the game. Irati, ecstatic, begins jumping up and down. You are furious and tell your father that she will not go because she broke Mother's crystal vase and she deserves to be grounded. "The child has to play," he says. You look at him in complete amazement, unable to react. You feel like you embody the punished generation.

While you are telling Martin what happened in the afternoon, he reads the newspaper and that drives you crazy. You are beside yourself. Every time he turns a page, you would snatch the paper from his hands and throw it out the window. Where is his respect for you? The consequences of breaking the vase have been greater than first thought. You hadn't felt this way in a long time. You feel as vulnerable as when you were an adolescent; more fragile than the vase itself.

You must end your daughter's awful fixation with soccer, whatever it takes. You do not believe that the bleach idea is so bad. All you need to do is to stain the jersey with bleach. Then you can lie to your daughter. After all, your parents planted many lies and fears in that weak head of yours. You have the right to do the same.

No matter what it takes, you must end Irati's obsession. It is not right for an eight-year-old girl to have such a devotion for a soccer team. Her friends love Hanna Montana or Hello Kitty. Those are normal girls, not like your daughter. You believe that the bleach idea deserves some careful consideration and, if you outline a script in your mind, it shouldn't be hard to carry out. As you are considering this idea, you accidentally drop your plastic water bottle. Martin asks what is the matter with you. You unload on him, almost running out of breath as you speak. You are trying so hard to stop your daughter's obsession and Martin is ignoring you.

He blurts his answer without lifting his eyes from the newspaper, like always, in complete calm: "Soccer is like any other passion, you can't eliminate it easily. If you bleach her jersey, she'll become a Real Madrid fan."

Once again, you think you have been impetuous. On the penalty shot that was set before you, you kicked the ball wide and your gaze raptly followed its trajectory: your husband calmly scored against you by kicking the ball right through the middle of the goal.

IXIAR ROZAS
Lasarte-Oria, 1972

I walk intertwining paths. I am an author, a video producer, a playwright, and a researcher. I have a doctorate in fine arts from the University of the Basque Country with a thesis considering voice and contemporary performance art. Developing from written texts, my work extends to: novels, narrations, poetry, scripts, texts for staged works, critical texts, and an array of materials that have been published in many languages and countries (Mexico, Italy, United Kingdom, United States, Portugal, Russia, and Slovenia.)

I am a founding member and an artistic director of the Periferia topaketa (Periphery encounters). These encounters organized in Italy and the Basque Country (2002–2007) addressed critical thinking in conjunction with artistic activity. I have directed *Humano caracol* productions, which are compilations of documentaries and micro-poetic archives dedicated to contemporary creators (2006–2011).

With writing as a point of departure, I have collaborated (and still collaborate) with the following choreographers and artists; Idoia Zabaleta (Gasteiz), Filipa Francisco (Lisboa), German Jauregui, (Bilbao/Brussels), Estela Lloves (Vigo/Berlin), Maria Muñoz and Pep Ramis (Mal Pelo, Girona) Maider Lopez (Donostia), Maite Arroitajauregi, Mursego

(Eibar).

After the birth of my son in 2010, (once again) immersed in life's "creases," I have written poems and short texts, and, following the voice I found in the novel *Negutegia* (2006) I am working on a longer piece. The story "A Draft" "Korrontea" which you have at hand was written at the beginning of 2000. If I were to write it now, it would be different, because I too am different.

⁂

Rozas has recently published *Beltzuria* (Black and white, 2014) pointing out the prominent role motherhood plays in it. In her words, at this moment she identifies more strongly with her recent work but, regrettably, Rozas published her new work about the time this anthology is going to press.

A Draft

Translated by Elizabeth Macklin and Linda White

"*E*xcuse me, would you close the door please?"
The woman isn't asking Abdou, but rather the man sitting next to the door. Sometimes the woman dozes off, but she awakes with a start when her head nods. When she opens her eyes, Abdou sees that they're watery, and he turns his gaze back to the window. once when her head nods, it lands on Abdou's shoulder. Her dark hair is very smooth, it looks like a child's, but the lines on her face make her look forty. She smells good, she has a unique scent. She doesn't wear cheap perfume like the village girls when they're out for boys. Abdou gently removes her head from his shoulder and leans it against the window.

The man sitting by the door has his eyes on a book. Every time the train is in a station, he lifts them to the window and sighs, as if he wants everything he's reading about to be reflected in the window. He also glances at the door from time to time, to make sure it's closed. He's dressed in black from head to foot. Black like the rain falling outside the window.

Ever since he was old enough to understand, Abdou had heard that rain has the power to grant wishes.

Before he got on the train, no one told him there would

be so much rain. They said where to go to catch the train and how long the trip would be, but not a word about the rain. Evidently, it hadn't seemed worth mentioning to those who gave him the information he needed to make the trip. No knowledge of rain was exchanged for the money he'd paid.

This detail is important to him though, because the success or failure of what he's about to do may lie in the rain. At least, if what he's heard about the power of the rain is true.

Abdou has just turned nineteen. He's headed for an unfamiliar city, to Paris, a name he has heard all his life on the tongues of his countrymen. He's traveling by train now, because they told him it was the surest way of avoiding unpleasant surprises. But before that, he traveled in every way possible, on foot, by ship—if an undersized launch could be called a ship—and in the back of a refrigerator truck. He traveled night and day in the company of other young men, all of them going in search of a better life. Fortunately, when he looked into their faces Abdou saw that he himself was different, because he was not searching for a better life. He was going to Paris for no other reason than to bring honor to his name.

It's been days since he bade farewell to his country, Mali. As he said goodbye, he looked into his mother's eyes and prayed that he might find his father. In his pocket, along with his father's photograph, he carried the address of a restaurant written on a piece of paper, the starting point of his search. It was said all Malians gathered there once a week, and they could certainly set him on his father's trail. That was his only hope because without their help, he didn't know where else to turn.

Word had come to him that they last saw Abdou's father in a Parisian train station. The restaurant owner reported that he was carrying a large suitcase, which could have meant he was leaving or arriving, but then the owner saw him catch a taxi, so he was coming to stay. Another compatriot in search of a better life, that's what the restaurant owner was thinking. By the time he got close to the taxi, it was pulling away. No chance to greet the new arrival. Nor had they seen him since. It was possible he had left the city, or perhaps had simply disappeared into its maze of streets and houses as do so many city dwellers. That was all they could say.

Abdou is certain that will not happen to him. He'll return home to his country. He's been thinking about that since he sat down on the train, everything made easier by its movement along the rails. or maybe he was thinking it because of a dozen other reasons, because he was mixed in with other people all traveling together. For now, Abdou is just another person in the compartment, different from the man and woman on either side of him but gazing out the window like someone who makes the journey every day, forgetting all about the photograph in his pocket. He paid for a ticket just like the others. He's not bad looking. He's wearing the beautiful shirt his mother bought him. only the darkness of his skin makes him stand out, but that's nothing to worry about, for in Paris there are many dark-skinned people like him.

Suddenly, the woman gets up, puts on her coat and goes into the corridor, holding a cell pone. The reader's eyes are glued to his book, glancing down now and then at the black suitcase between his feet. The dark-haired woman is beautiful, she's wearing red lipstick and is elegantly dressed. She folds her arms across her middle, as if her coat were not enough to warm her body. She takes a few drags on the cigarette and returns to the compartment, just as another young man enters. If he were dark-skinned, he'd look a lot like Abdou. But there's a big difference between the two of the them. Unlike Abdou, the newcomer chose his destination randomly.

"Is this seat free?" asks the young man, glancing around the compartment.

He asks with a smile. The three of them nod yes, the woman mechanically, Abdou pleasantly, and the reader without lifting his eyes from his book. He only glances sideways as the rough-looking newcomer enters. The newcomer carries a case. So does the woman, but his isn't a briefcase, it's a case for a musical instrument, a guitar, a violin, or a viola, one of those.

For a second, it feels like Abdou and the young man are all alone in the compartment, the way they look at each other, long and hard, taking each other's measure. Then Abdou turns his gaze back to the window. Although in his country it was relatively common for men to sleep with men, Abdou loves women. He would be happy to spend night after night embracing the sweet-smelling brunette at his side, nibbling at her delicate lips.

The compartment door is left open again.

"Excuse me, would you close the door please? There's a draft, and I wouldn't want to get a chill," says the woman as pleasantly as possible.

She folds her arms across her middle again. Her eyes are closing, as if she guessed Abdou's thoughts and wants to flee from them. The landscape outside the window is green. That generous landscape whizzing by is so different from the stingy flatlands of his own country. The landscape there looks like the wrinkled skin of an old man. Here it seems fluffy, like a baby's curly hair.

There are so many things Abdou does not understand.

Why are there so many obstacles to getting anywhere? Why does he have to move like a snake in the dirt, risking his life, if the big nations have already stolen everything they need from his country?

And the one question that stands out above all others: Why have you done all of this to us?

That's a question Abdou would like to ask the others in the train compartment. Would they have any answers? But then, who is he to barge into the lives of such peaceful people? He prefers to believe that one of these days everything will be easier, although ever since he was old enough to understand, he heard that power grows on the backs of the small, and his country could still become much more diminished. Nevertheless, he truly believes that something is changing in his own life, and it's better to believe in small things than big ones. In order to change the big things, you have to begin with the small ones, and that's just what he'll do when he finds his father's trail.

Perhaps the rain will help him.

It was raining that morning he woke up and found his mother crying. It was no wonder he remembered that rain, for in his country it only rains once or twice a year. Add the fact that his father left home that morning, and Abdou was bound to remember the rain. A father leaves for good once in a lifetime, or maybe twice, but if he comes back and leaves a second time there is no third chance. That's what Abdou had heard since he was old enough to understand.

❧ ❦ ❧

That's why, in the beginning, Abdou thought his father would return and his mother's tears were caused by something else. He thought she was crying for joy because his father had gone away to bring back a baby. His mother's hidden desire was to have another baby. Abdou's hidden desire was revealed when he spoke to her sweetly, saying, "Don't worry, he'll be home by nightfall."

Abdou spoke tenderly to his mother in his capacity as eldest brother. It was his duty. However, he was unable to soothe her distress. Tears darkened her face with the same power of the water that furrowed the dry earth. Her hands trembled and so did the paper she held. The silence was so pervasive he could even hear the paper trembling. At last, staring into space, his mother ended the silence.

"He's gone. He's gone and left us, Abdou."

She appended her son's name at the end, for he was the only hope left to her. Abdou returned to his bedroom, scowling at the rain through the open window. Smoke seemed to rise from the earth, a tussle between the heat and the rain. Smoke poured out of the bedroom, too. Abdou had rolled a cigarette and was smoking furiously.

He was only fifteen then. Four years passed before the morning when he learned his mother was sick.

"Go look for him, Abdou," she insisted. "I don't want to leave you all by yourselves when I die."

She was speaking of her seven sons and daughters. As the eldest, Abdou knew that his mother had never spoken with such grim determination before. Something was about to happen. He could lose no time. He would do everything in his power to find his father.

᪣ ᪴ ᪵

The woman gets up from her seat, and the noise brings Abdou back to the train. She picks up her small black case and goes into the corridor. She takes her phone, presses the buttons, and waits. Then nervously, she begins to speak as if her life were draining from her with every utterance. Somberly, she ends the call. Then she makes another, more serenely. A smile appears on her face while she waits for someone to answer. From her case, she takes out a diary and opens it.

Abdou is not the only one watching the woman. The reader watches her, too. But the newcomer is a prisoner of his own thoughts, or perhaps of the instrument in his case. The woman ends the second call. She picks up her case, lights another cigarette, and moves along the corridor. She takes a long drag and stands looking out the window. Lights from the highway outside are reflected in her face, light and shadow, light and shadow. She's one of those women who thinks twice before making decisions. Another drag on the cigarette, another thought.

"Excuse me, would you close the door please? There's a draft."

The words hang in the air. She has a weighty voice that gives each word immense importance, unlike the lighter, quicker voice of the newcomer. Just as he randomly chose Paris over any other destination, his voice made one word seem like any other. He hasn't spoken again since he entered the compartment.

"Are you married? Do you have any children?"

Abdou would like to ask those questions. He'd like to know if having a husband was the reason for her teary eyes, if she had just called him. The reader now gazes at Abdou's old traveling bag as if trying to guess what is inside. But he never could because it is full of the mementos and photos that Abdou had brought along to convince his father to return home.

"If you rekindle his memories, he'll come back," his mother announced as she packed her chosen mementos into his bag.

"And if I don't find him, mother, what then?" Abdou asks himself now.

When the woman reenters the compartment, the reader returns to his book as if embarrassed to have been looking at Abdou. It crosses Abdou's mind that the woman might be having her period. Abdou's sense of smell is highly developed and he knows that menstruating women have a different scent. But the sweet smell of her perfume wins out and he can detect no other. He'd have to be closer to her to be sure. If she puts her head on his shoulder again, he will inhale more deeply. For now, he concentrates totally on what he's about to say.

"Will it be long before we arrive?" Abdou dares to ask.

❧ ❦ ❧

He believes that questions are often a way of getting closer to strangers. The newcomer shakes his head no with a smile. The other two, however, seem far, far away from the train compartment. Abdou feels that quite a few hours have passed since the departure, so it's possible that it won't be long now, as the newcomer suggests. He takes the photo of his father out of his pocket and dares to ask another question, almost afraid to breathe.

"Do any of you know him?" Timidly. "He's my father."

The three of them turn to look at the photo. Silently, they examine it. Abdou needs only the faintest positive sign to feel his journey is not useless, but the silence continues. At last, with a hopeless gesture, the newcomer says he's sorry, but he hasn't been in the city for years.

The woman remarks, "Finding someone in Paris is as impossible as believing in fate."

Again, her words hang heavy in the air. She glances sideways at the photo, at the undeniable resemblance between father and son.

The woman would take pleasure in telling Abdou that the man might not be his father. He can only be sure of his mother. He'll never know if his father is for real. That's the way life is in big cities like Paris. She would also tell him to go home to his country if he wants to avoid the city's clutches. And while she's thinking that, their eyes meet and linger for the first time. Sparks fly. She thinks she could lose herself in his lips for a long night.

"No, I've never seen him. I'm very sorry, very sorry," as if the repetition it will convince herself, and she shakes her head no.

Her eyes are an unknown color, since for dark-skinned people no color is more unfamiliar than blue, like the Mali sky on a dark night. Abdou has known that, too, for a long time.

Silence descends on the compartment, a silence broken only by the sound of the rails, shutting out even the smallest word of cheer.

The newcomer begins to whistle. He could take his instrument from its case and start playing right now. The reader has his eyes on his book, and the woman looks out the window. She combs her fingers through her long hair, opening wide spaces between the strands. Through them, Abdou sees that the light from the window is brighter now. They are undoubtedly entering a city much larger than any they have passed through thus far. As soon as he's off the train, he'll have a taxi driver take him to the address on the paper he carries.

The train is slowing down. The woman uses a hand mirror to touch up her makeup. Then she stands up, leaves the compartment, and starts talking on the phone. Just as before, she makes the first call with a taut face, and the second with a smile.

She still hasn't returned to her seat. She's standing in the corridor, thoughtful, watching the night lights of the city. Abdou scoots closer to the window. He sees the iron roof of the station and, reflected in the glass, his own exhausted face, limned with the fear that a few days in this city will turn into months, and the months into years. That's what has happened to everyone who left Mali.

The newcomer caresses the side of his instrument case, eager to put his fingers to the strings. The reader closes his book and sighs, for he won't be able to read again until he's finally home. or perhaps he is bored with the book, maybe it has failed to capture his attention. The woman in the corridor lights a cigarette.

The train slows even more. Abdou sees the large station clock. It's ten p.m. But he wasn't expecting what he saw beneath the clock. They told him the train was the safest way to travel, that nothing would happen to him, but they also told him to go by night. He hoped the shirt his mother bought him would make him less conspicuous. Beads of perspiration run down his temples. Plainclothes policemen are on the platform waiting for the moment they'll make an arrest.

The woman reenters the compartment. She looks straight at Abdou as if to ask how he will avoid the police. The reader stows his book in his bag and the newcomer doesn't even notice the police presence. His gaze and consciousness are elsewhere.

The woman offers Abdou a cigarette. Their hands touch as she brings the lighter flame toward him. Abdou, however, is unable to smile a thank you. The woman lifts her suitcase from the metal shelf above her head. The reader also picks up his bag, a wheeled suitcase. The newcomer cradles his instrument case under his arm.

But Abdou remains in his seat. If it were raining the rain that grants wishes, he would beg the train not to stop, to retrace all the miles that have brought him here. But the station is huge and the sheltering roof prevents him from seeing whether it's raining.

The three others move toward the door of the car and wait to see who will be first to step through. The sudden light of the station reveals Abdou's fear.

The train has come to a complete stop. Abdou has no choice but to stand and sling his bag over his shoulder. The woman pauses and lets the reader go ahead of her. On the platform, one of the policemen peers intently at everyone who gets off the train. The reader goes down the steps, and the newcomer follows him, casting a glance at Abdou as if wanting him to know that at last he understands everything. Abdou wants to retrace his steps, but it's too late. It's the woman's turn to descend the steps and Abdou follows her as his eyes catch the policeman's shrewd smile. Then, in a split second, the woman takes Abdou's arm.

"My husband is quite slow," she says to the policeman, without hesitation. "Come, darling, our little girl is waiting." She plants a light kiss on Abdou's cheek but says no more. They descend from the car arm in arm. Abdou is speechless. He can't believe what is happening. The woman holds tightly to his arm. He is under her control, entirely at her service.

The suspicious policeman watches the couple for a second, a word on the tip of his tongue. But instead he says something to his partner, and they go on with their surveillance.

The reader sees it all. He almost said something, but instead prefers to watch the momentary couple disappear through the station entrance. He has never read anything like this in his books. The newcomer sits down on a random bench, waiting.

As they leave the station, Abdou notices that it's raining. The woman makes sure the police are no longer watching, then releases his arm. He smiles at her, a smile full of gratitude and instant loyalty. They share a goodbye glance.

The woman gives the man who waits for her a light kiss on the lips. They get on a motorcycle and disappear in the distance.

Abdou hails a cab and takes the address from his pocket. The driver is unwelcoming at first, but as soon as he sees that Abdou has the money to pay for the ride, he tells him to get in. Abdou looks at his bag. He looks at the leather seat of the taxi. The rain washes the sweat from his temples and he climbs into the taxi. He takes his seat and shows the driver the photo of his father. The city rushes past the windows.

Arantxa Urretabizkaia Bejarano

Donostia, 1947

*A*rantxa Urretabizkaia Bejarano (1947) was born in Donostia-San Sebastián and lives in the village of Hondarribi. After having worked in different fields, she has been a journalist for more than thirty years. Her experience includes working at ETB-Basque TV, the Basque radio station and newspapers such as *El Diario Vasco*, *El Correo*, *El Mundo*, and *Deia*.

She published her first literary work, a collection of poems titled *San Pedro bezperaren ondokoak* (The aftermath of St. Peter's Eve), in 1972. Since then she has concentrated on novels: *Zergatik Panpox?* (Why, cutie? 1979), *Saturno* (Saturn, 1987), *Koaderno gorria* (1998; *The Red Notebook*, English translation 2008), and *3 Mariak* (The three Marys, 2010), among others. The short story "Espero zaitudalako" ("Because I'm Expecting You) was published in *Aspaldian espero zaitudalako ez nago sekula bakarrik* (I'm never alone because I'm expecting you, 1983).

Because I'm Expecting You

*I*t all began at Christmas, during the second holiday season Coro spent at the convent. Coro confided in me that, as a child, Christmas had never been very meaningful for her: parents, siblings, carols, fish soup, and turrón accompanied by too many demands. Apparently it was always difficult for Coro to feel happy when her surroundings required community happiness. Indeed, her desire to escape her surroundings had been the force that brought her to the convent. Although what happened later might suggest otherwise, the truth was that she could not recognize herself amid such a sea of feelings and interests.

It would take only five minutes conversing with Coro to confirm that the convent was a hideout for her. The stone walls surrounding the convent kept the world away without restricting her access to the outside, yet these walls provided cherished shade to neutralize external assaults.

As the Mother Superior informed me, nothing out-of-the-ordinary happened during the first year-and-a-half of her stay. If anything, Coro had shown a remarkable ability to adapt to everyday convent-life. The fact is that, even after the story broke out, many of the nuns still saw Coro as just a small-town, devout, young woman. A humble and loveable person prone to prayer and meditation. She was the lamb that everyone wanted to protect.

Coro did not feel any kind of pressure at the convent. However, what happened to her did not and, in my opinion, will not ever, surprise her. For Coro the story did not begin that exact day, her dream just happened to come true that Christmas.

The day before Christmas, in the morning while on her way from the garden to the convent-house, she saw a baby Jesus figurine resting on the small table in front of one of the dining room's balconies. At that precise moment the room appeared to Coro like a long, black tunnel with a light lingering above and illuminating the baby. But in reality, the main dining room is a wide chamber, painted in white and flanked by three big balconies. The tunnel and its surrounding light were part of Coro's imagination: for her, the world inside the convent became real based on the imagery found in sacred scriptures.

And so, the day before Christmas, under a dim but hardly a forlorn light, she noticed a baby Jesus figurine on a table, lying on a bed of straw "not sawdust," as Coro insisted in her account again and again; "he rested on fresh golden straw, with no cradle." In Coro's eyes, the figurine was made of stone, but even before holding it in my hands, I could see at a glance that it was made of plaster. It was the kind that can be found by the dozens at any store. It happened to be the figurine that Coro's aunts had given her when she entered the convent. The community had put it in storage because one of the Baby's hands was cracked.

Coro explained that when she saw the baby, she stopped in her tracks. A baby made of stone with his knee bent slightly and who raised his opposite little hand in a hesitant blessing.

He looked so real. The cold in the convent, which numbed Coro's hands, made the baby shiver; yet he displayed a courageous smile. Coro described his smile to me with special emphasis, perhaps because it was a bit crooked or maybe it just seemed crooked because it was under a pair of eyes that were even more crooked. In Coro's mind the clumsiness of his gaze wasn't the result of an unskilled and impatient artist, it was rather the representation of someone like Coro herself, abandoned, cast-off. However, since I've gotten to know those around Coro, I haven't seen anyone who loved those crooked eyes as much as she did.

Coro hasn't been able to explain what happened to her in that moment nor does she understand the questions or the ruckus that followed. After she first saw the baby she felt the need to spend as much time as possible next to him. At every break from her chores and prayers, she stood before him, in stillness, with no need to touch his painted skin. As Coro told me, she needed to be next to him because that stone figurine was sweeter and purer than anything she could ever have pictured in her mind while working in the garden or praying in the chapel.

The other nuns and the Mother Superior hardly noticed anything out of the ordinary. Coro was the youngest among them and everyone loved her. They did not become worried about what was brewing inside Coro's head until much later.

That Christmas, Coro did not face any restrictions. She gazed at the baby intently, with no logical thoughts flooding her mind. She would spend half an hour contemplating the inside of his arm or the blessing hand or waiting for a curl to come undone. By the time Christmas was over, she thought she knew every inch of his body. She would even describe in great detail what was not apparent: the cold softness of his skin, the tender bones in his back. She did not touch him, not because she did not dare to, but because she did not feel the need.

When I asked her if she had ever thought about what was under the whitish cloth that covered him from his waist to his thigh, she looked at me with such surprise and in such a serene way that I dropped that line of questioning. Coro did not understand, after all the confusion had passed, why the nuns, the bishop and I had worried.

Apparently, five days or so after Christmas, once they had stored the baby away, all it took to picture his crooked gaze was for her to close her eyes. Little by little, as time passed, she began losing her ability to do so. After a few months, it became too difficult to envision the baby any longer.

For a long while, nothing special happened, except for a few tender words said to her by a nun or a few racing heartbeats when she would come across the image of the baby Jesus in some book. But for her heart to quicken, the baby had to be alone because when the baby was with the Virgin Mary, nothing happened. The imagination has its own prerequisites and rules.

When the second Christmas came around, if we are to believe her account, Coro didn't expect anything. The presence of the baby caught her by surprise once more. The Mother Superior was not worried. When she took the baby out and placed it in front of the middle balcony, she did not feel any anxiety.

It was wintertime and the balcony windows were fogged. If we accept as true the light Coro saw, it must have been a clear day, a resplendent, winter midday. When she entered the dining room, she saw the baby backlit; he looked paler than the year before. I found out later that the Mother Superior had washed the Baby in milk to get rid of all the dust that he had accumulated in his crevices. Coro didn't think that the yearlong, short-lived love had changed anything. She knew it was the same baby, yet the knee seemed to display a new movement. The baby was neither alive nor dead. He just lay there. That was all.

This time Coro began to deceive the rest of the sisters in order to spend as much time as possible in the dining room. Tricks without mischievousness, the kind one respects because the heart is in charge. It wasn't that she refused to leave the baby alone. The need to be close to the baby was Coro's and not the baby's. The long, humid, dark corridor was well aware of Coro's love.

She quickly noticed details she had overlooked until then. For example, the tender dimples on his knees or the sweet dip where his neck and chest came together. Such discoveries were the highlights of her day, though for her, the crooked gaze never lost its predominance.

Until the following year, she did not feel the need to touch him. She would stand before him and look at him. Standing up, as the Mother Superior would emphasize, because she considered it very important that while all this happened, Coro never knelt down.

It didn't seem like anyone paid any particular attention to this story involving the baby. Furthermore, I can't say that the Mother Superior and especially the older nuns disliked the situation; they enjoyed it but in the same manner unimportant things are loved. Devotion could not interfere with daily chores.

When Christmas was over, Coro felt a new uneasiness. How did she learn so little this time? A week later she couldn't remember the shadows on his flesh any longer, the movement of his gestures; he had been reduced to nothing but a whitish mass.

As time passed, she found herself unable to experience the peace she felt before and time elapsed with only one objective: Christmas. At first, she tried to get interested in the baby that the Virgin in the chapel held in her arms, but in vain, perhaps because she could not see him up close or because after all, it wasn't the same baby.

When the chores took her to the garden in summer, she felt a blue emptiness inside her every time she climbed the bitter steps leading to the dining room.

When the baby appeared for the third time, Coro had already anticipated his presence. She began expecting him in early December as if believing that the arrival of the month reaffirmed their relationship. A few days before Christmas she felt an unfamiliar, anguishing sensation in the pit of her stomach. It wasn't pain but anxiety, an uneasiness that receded when she saw his neck propped up on the straw.

On that occasion, as soon as she paused her eyes on him, she felt the urge to touch his helpless body. She had waited for him for so many months. As she told me in a voice drowned in sadness, she hadn't been able to imagine the Baby since the previous Christmas, no matter how persistently she tried to look for him in the garden among the flowers.

Coro did not touch the baby right then. She could not decide — she told me later in the languid tone often adopted by those revealing a burdensome problem — which part of the Baby to touch first. Should she kiss him on the eyes or caress the poor, little, hidden thumb of his right hand?

The Baby seemed softer, more needy, as women who will never bear children might see him. After observing him carefully, she noticed two small creases on his shoulders together with the little dimples on his knees. And she wondered if that blessing gesture wasn't rather a sign of him trying to reach out to someone.

Year after year, the depth of emotion the Baby stirred in her intensified. When Coro explained what happened during the third Christmas, she used words and inflections often heard in radio drama, she paused and carefully modulated her voice.

In previous years, the Mother Superior was not worried about the time Coro diverted from her chores but this time around, as Christmas unfolded, she came to face philosophical quandaries. The Second Vatican Council did not happened in vain when she was a novice. Surely, the scandal that would erupt if the news of a saint among them came out, would not help her convent. The Mother Superior had learned the hard way that as soon as emotions sprang, they had to be tamed at once.

They forbade Coro to enter the dining room outside of regular hours. Even in the bitter cold winter dusks of North Navarre, she would spend hours under the dining room balconies. Then the dining room truly seemed to her to be at the end of a dark tunnel, the white light at its mouth definitely felt painful.

Perhaps, thrust by one of those early evenings and before attending prayer time at nine, she dared to enter the dining room and caress the baby, as if she had been lured to respect and follow a magic force. She touched his waist, under the side of the blessing hand. That's apparently when Coro's purple, stiff, frozen hands warmed up a little, yet there was no electrical jolt of any kind. They became closer to each other, that was all. That is when Coro realized, as she told me later, that the reason she came to the convent was to seek those moments. The nuns had not become aware of what had happened.

Such had been the climax of this love story; a time that exposed happy and blissful feelings, an act of undisturbed hope.

That year the Mother Superior put the baby away on Three Kings Day while she tried to decide if she should consult with someone about the episode. Truth be told, Coro's serene demeanor helped ease her concerns. Besides, young people forget things easily. All of us who have met Coro understand the Mother Superior's relaxed attitude.

Coro's devotion was rewarded. Throughout the year the baby did not completely vanish from her mind, the hand that she had worn out by looking at it so much would be replaced with his back or neck in her imagination. Every night she fell asleep cradling the baby's memory in her arms, waiting to see him in her dreams. But the baby did not come to her in her dreams, at least Coro couldn't remember.

By the time the fourth Christmas came around, the Mother Superior had pondered displaying the baby as she did every year or pretending she forgot. Since Coro's work and devotion raised no suspicion at all throughout the year, the Mother Superior did not find any reason to worry. She went ahead and displayed the baby though later than other times, the very morning of Christmas Day. The Mother Superior and Coro remember it well.

For Coro Christmas Eve wasn't the day of the baby's birth. For her the baby no longer lived in the liturgical world. The Bishop became aware of it instantly, as soon as he began talking with Coro. As the Bishop told me when he asked me to be part of this case, of course it was God but like one of the gods that were worshiped before the times of Jesus Christ.

The fact is that on Christmas Day around noon, the baby lay on the straw as always.

Coro's devotion time had been limited from the start: a few minutes before and after meals, until the Mother Superior determined to end the session. Coro was unable to eat under the spell of his presence. She wasn't able to love the baby properly in the midst of all the nuns. She hadn't identified all the details she found in previous years much less have a chance to find new treasures. His gaze, though as crooked and teary as always, seemed hazy now. Coro thought that the baby too could be suffering from lack of intimacy.

The situation was such that though many nuns, including the Mother Superior, had began considering even the wind to be threatening, Coro could not understand the prohibition. She marveled at the reaction they all had and not at what had provoked it, her attraction to baby Jesus. She hasn't been able to understand whom she hurt by keeping her devotion to the baby.

When the scandal broke and extended to what now seems forever, it was as if a play was cast with all the wrong actors, as if astronauts would show up in a western. The emotion that Coro felt for the baby filled the air but in the same manner as when rain falls and inundates the ground; the earth remains as helpless in the storm as under the sun.

Even after talking to the Mother Superior, a priest, and the bishop, Coro hasn't come to her senses. She listens to what others tell her with her eyes wide open, without displaying any pride or sense of guilt. She told me effortlessly, forgetting nothing, what by now she could narrate by heart having repeated it so many times. She stored it away and, as if she were an actress, used suspiciously happy sentences. Nevertheless, as in Greek Tragedies, under every rhetorical device there is an emotion, real pain or happiness. I can remember details in Coro's narration that aroused such feelings within me, bringing them to life.

At first, the Mother Superior interpreted the situation as an out-dated case of mysticism. But since then, she has been given a more reassuring explanation. The bishop, and the Mother Superior under his influence, undoubtedly believe that for Coro the baby is the substitute for the children that she will never bear. But I'm not so sure. The main issue in this case is not Coro's need to protect the baby. Coro never believed that the baby needed a mother. In my opinion, for Coro the baby is more a lover than a son.

During the last Christmas season, on New Years Eve, after they had finished dinner and their prayers, an hour after all the nuns had gone to bed, Coro could not fall asleep.

She felt the urge to go to the dining room. Since the innitial sighting, this was the first time she felt frightened. It was one thing to fool the nuns in the day time and quite another to get up in the middle of the night. A soft voice echoed the scream that was unleashed inside her, ordering her to go to the dining room. Coro has never been one for extremes.

It must have been about two in the morning when she realized that in a few days they would take the baby away from her. She got up and went out to the corridor, barefoot, wearing nothing but her nightgown. She had completely forgotten the interval between when she thought they would hide the baby from her and when she arrived at the dining room door.

As soon as she held the baby, she realized she was not in her room, in bed. She is still able to explain the smallest detail of what happened after. From the blue light entering the room through the window to the silver color of the straw under the baby. As I was able to confirm later, that night the moon was in front of the balcony and it was a clear and damp night. One of those nights that make the moon look like cold fire.

As soon as she held the baby in her arms and before she had the opportunity to enjoy his sweet smile under the dim light, the subdued light of the dining room switched on. It was the Mother Superior, praying the Hail Holy Queen and dressed in her full habit.

As the Mother Superior told everyone later, Coro looked as if she had gone insane. Nevertheless, she did not offer any resistance when she handed him over.

BEGOÑA BILBAO ALBONIGA

Bermeo, 1932–2005

*B*egoña Bilbao Alboniga completed her elementary studies in her town's Karmelita school but did not get a
chance to further her education. As a child she lived through
the Spanish Civil War. From an early age she was an avid
reader but instead of going to school she learned sewing and
embroidery. Later in life she opened two tailor shops. But her
love for reading and the Basque language led her to complete
a bachelor's degree in Basque Philology. She graduated from
the University of Deusto in 1982 at fifty-five years of age.

After that, her commitment to the Basque language became even stronger and she began writing prolifically. From
1982 to 2001 she won fifteen literary prizes, among them,
The Irun Hiria award, which was given to the story included
in this collection. During these years, she published sixteen
works, mainly short stories, except for two essays: "Ber-
meoko euskara kresaltsua: Aditza eta fonetika" (Bermeo's
coastal Basque: Verb system and phonetics, 2002) and "Ber-
meoko esamolde eta esaera kresaltsuak" (Proverbs and sayings from Bermeo, 2003). She also wrote song lyrics. The
first song she wrote was about Palestine, sung by her daughter Analupe, and her last work, her only novel also had Pales-

tine as a theme, *Palestina, zure mina* (Palestine, your sorrow, 2004). She died a year after the publication of her novel.

Spilled Water Cannot Be Re-Gathered

*T*here has been a car accident on the Bilbao road, at the place they call the "Curve of Death." A twenty year old was killed while driving. No one knows how it happened, he must have gone off the road and plunged down the cliff. Those that saw the body say he was disfigured. There is so much misfortune in that family! The accident victim is the great-grandson of Josepa whose nickname in the village is White Skirt. This is devastating news for a ninety-two-year-old woman. She no longer has any family; she is the last one left. But this is not the first bad news Josepa has ever received. She has experienced all kinds of family misfortune through-out her life, and this accident might well be the last one she will have to endure. Two years ago, her great-granddaughter died too, the sister of the boy killed in the accident. A group of youngsters, Karmele among them, went to the island known as Izaro when something mysterious happened. Her friend said that she disappeared during the night and no one has heard from Karmele since. The two siblings were orphans and lived with Josepa. Their parents also died under tragic circumstances. Their father, while working at sea, got caught in the boat's motor and was left with no arms and amputated legs. He died soon after. At that time, their mother was pregnant and miscarried as a result of the devastating news. She never discharged all the babys' remains and her blood got infected, rotting her from the inside out. This woman's parents did not have normal deaths either. Her father fell overboard on a stormy day and though they searched for him soon after the fall, they were unsuccessful. He was found a month later among the seaside rocks, his eyes eaten by fish. The story goes that his wife killed herself, though it was never proven. When they realized she had gone missing, they began looking for her and found her slippers on top of the rock known as Tonpoi Handi. They found her cardigan at the base. Everyone thinks she either fell from the rocks or jumped. Her body was never found because of the strong sea currents and whirlpools in the area.

If this family were destined to suffer a curse placed on them forty-two years earlier by Josepa's friend Mikela, the full measure has been realized. Josepa has not only suffered the curse, but has witnessed it too. This ninety-two year old woman has had to see and endure it all.

Mikela and Josepa were friends. They were both married and lived the typical fishing village life. Josepa had two sons and a daughter and Mikela had a daughter. Their children were grown; Josepa's youngest son was already eighteen. The daughters of both women, Luzia and Karmen, were friends too. It was natural that, after being childhood friends, their friendship would continue as adults. Since they lived on the same street, they saw one another often and kept a close relationship. They also happened to work at the same cannery. Mikela and Josepa worked at the port. As daughters of fishingboat–owning families, they worked in the business.

At that time, even though the families owned fishing boats, they were not wealthy. They did not lack for the basics but, in order to survive, they needed all the family members' earnings, no matter how big or small their contribution. It was wartime and food was scarce, which meant that even working hard, it was difficult to make a comfortable living.

Luzia and Karmen were regular girls, physically and intellectually. They were plain and there was nothing about them that set them apart from the rest of the girls. Truth be told, they did not have the means to stand out. They did not have much extra money to afford beautiful clothing. They had to be their own hairdressers because there was only one shop in town and it fell on one's own ability to look more elegant than the rest. It was impossible to find makeup and if someone got ahold of lipstick, they had to apply it away from home because, in those days, parents forbade young women to wear any trace of makeup. Decent people did not use makeup, prostitutes did. In small towns, wealthy women did not wear makeup either, it was taboo. That was why it was difficult for Luzia and Karmen to spruce up or change their look a bit. They only were able to change their hairdos. On weekends, they would buy a bunch of hairpins and look for pieces of electric cables to use as curlers. They ended up with their heads full of waves and clumps of hair held by pieces of cable, which had to be covered before going to bed. They had to be careful not to move much while in bed so the waves and bunches would not come undone. It was rather uncomfortable to go to sleep like that but they were going to be seen in town on Sunday and that required putting up with all that discomfort. The next day, on Sunday, they had forgotten about the inconvenience. When the time came to get ready for the town dance, after taking off the homemade curlers, they confirmed that they looked pretty good and both would go out to look for the rest of their girlfriends.

In winter, the dance was held from six to eight in the upper plaza of town while in summer it took place in Lamera and went until nine. The band played two pieces every half hour, for a total of eight or twelve, plus an encore. Between pieces, dancers got as close as possible to the objects of their desire, so that when the music resumed they would naturally be placed to dance with them.

But Luzia and Karmen's friendship soon shattered. Everything changed when both fell in love with Esteban. Esteban was a fisherman. Even though he was average looking, he was known in town as a good and hard-working young man. He had caught the attention of many young women. But he had been spending a lot of time with Luzia and Karmen, though no one knew which one he liked best.

This is how both young women, little by little, turned into rivals and began doing their best to attract Esteban. Luzia was slow, while Karmen was quicker, less timid. She approached Esteban more easily and used any excuse to get close to him and strike up conversation. This daring worked in her favor and she took full advantage of it to dazzle him. Luzia on the other hand did not get in Karmen's way and only enjoyed Esteban's company when he approached her.

Both mothers clearly saw that the boy would be a good catch for their daughters. Sadly for Karmen, Esteban ended up choosing Luzia. That was when the real trouble began between the two friends. Karmen accused Luzia of stealing her boyfriend, and Luzia, trying to avoid any confrontation with Karmen, did not act very receptive to Esteban's attentions. So they pretended to be friends during and after work, as if nothing had changed.

Although Karmen kept her angry feelings bottled up inside, it was obvious she did not resign herself to be second best. She felt like she had to do something and began plotting to break up the relationship between Esteban and Luzia. Esteban was out of town so she could take her time; there was no need to rush. It was summer, the time when fishing boats stayed at sea for long periods of time. This allowed Luzia and Karmen to calm down a little and, while not forgetting their problems, to put them aside for a time.

September arrived and with it the village festivals. All boats were home, moored in the port. The excitement and yearning were palpable all over town. It was the eve of Andra Mari, the day of the village patron saint, and Karmen chose that day to carry out her plan. After she carefully thought out her strategy, she went to the river, carrying a bucket full of clothes on her head. In those days, it was customary to wash clothes in the river. And Karmen knew where to find Esteban — he lived on the path to the river — and she knew what time she might stumble upon him. On that very same road, she could find something else she needed to achieve her plan; the slaughterhouse was in the same direction, on Erribera Street where she was headed. Every Friday they slaughtered cattle and discarded their bloody hides behind the building. Karmen was headed there. It was five in the afternoon and no one was in the slaughterhouse or its surroundings. There were a few children playing nearby but no one else in sight. The children did not worry her. She soiled the clothes she carried in her bucket with blood and walked furtively to the road Esteban would take, making sure she did not call attention to herself. She did not have to wait long before she spotted Esteban coming down the road, carrying a fish basket, wearing the typical dark blue fisherman work pants and shirt. To Karmen, he was better looking than ever.

"Good afternoon, Esteban."

"Karmen? What brings you here?"

"I'm headed to the river to wash these clothes. They are not very dirty and it won't take me long."

"It must be important if you are headed to the river this late. Yes, it must really be urgent because you usually don't do your wash this late in the day."

"You said it. You're right. It's urgent. I shouldn't tell you but, since I'm your best friend and you won't doubt my word, I'll tell you."

"What do you need to tell me?"

"Don't forget, Esteban, that I'm your closest friend and I love you very much, like a sister, of course. I'll be happy to help you."

"Will you let me know what's going on already?"

"Well . . . Luzia's had a miscarriage. Her mother is upset and beside herself. That's why I'm headed to the river to wash her bed sheets."

The bucket she had earlier carried on her head, she now placed on the ground and showed Esteban the bloodstained sheets. He did not know what to say; he was speechless. It was not possible. How? Whose baby was it? Who was the father? He knew for a fact that he was not. He never laid with her. They kissed, they caressed, but they did not go beyond that.

"But how is this possible? Who has she been with?"

"No one knows, not even her mother. This morning Mikela came to our house screaming that her daughter was dying. Saying that her daughter had a horrible stomach ache and that something was very wrong with her. We rushed there and we found Luzia on her bed, half dead. And that's when it happened. Suddenly she began bleeding and by the time the doctor arrived everything was over."

Esteban could hardly stand. He finally said:

"I'll demand an explanation from her. She owes me an explanation."

"If I were you, I wouldn't. She's kept it quiet from everyone. She's betrayed you, deceived you. As the best friend of you both, I know how much you love her. But she hasn't told me anything either and if this hadn't happened, I'm not sure how far she would've gone. Sincerely, if I were you, I wouldn't say anything."

"Yes, you're right." And without further commotion, they went their separate ways.

Luzia felt full of anticipation. Town festivals were always a reason for excitement. For the last few hours, she kept ironing her prettiest clothes again and again, and polishing and shining her shoes. It was the first day of the festival and she was waiting for Esteban's call. She was ready to join him in the barn as soon as she heard him whistle. But it was ten and Esteban was nowhere to be found. What happened? Was he sick? If that were the case, he would have let her know. But there was no message or sign of Esteban and she had to remain home.

The following day, she spent the early hours of the day doing housework and running Mother's errands. She needed to be ready at noon to go to the town concert. It was customary to bring a band from out of town to perform a daily, noon-hour concert. All the town youth met there. When Luzia was finally ready, she went to get Karmen. She called from downstairs, like always, but no one answered. She thought it a little strange because whoever got ready first went to get the other. Not finding her at home really surprised her. Nevertheless, she did not dwell on it and went to the plaza alone, hoping to find her friend there.

Karmen was already there with their group of friends.

Luzia went toward them but when they saw her approaching, they ignored her and took off the opposite way. Though Luzia was puzzled, she once again advanced in their direction and once again they did the same, walking away from her. Just then, a group of guys passed by her and she realized it was Esteban's group. Esteban was among them and when he walked by, he acknowledged her with a nod but did not stop.

Luzia was perplexed. Earlier he did not show up and did not explain why, and now, when they crossed paths, instead of asking her what time they should go out in the afternoon, he walked by without uttering a word. It was not fair. Even when they were with their own group of friends, they would always get together to chat about something. But now it did not happen, moreover, Esteban seemed angry, at least that was the impression Luzia got. She did not know what to do or what to think. She was not going to stay by herself; it was not appropriate for a young woman to be alone at a town concert. Should she go home? Should she look for a friend? But who? It would be best to go home. And that is what she did.

"You're early. Are you sick?" asked her mother.

"No, I'm not sick but, something strange happened with my friends and Esteban," and she told her mother what happened.

"What's happened for them to act like that?"

"I don't know, Mother, it's strange but I'll find out soon."

Luzia left the house. It was almost two in the afternoon and the concert had just finished. She waited for the concert to end to ask Karmen about what happened earlier. When she saw her walking down the street, she did not hesitate and walked in her direction.

"Karmen, I need to know what's going on."

"What do you mean? I don't know what you're talking

about."

"Don't pretend you don't know. What you did at the concert is not normal."

"Well, normal or not, from today on you'll need to find new friends because you are no longer coming with us."

"Why not?"

"You should know. Leave me alone. Bye!"

"But, listen to me please! What have I done?"

"You should know. Don't talk to me anymore!" and without saying one more word, Karmen kept on walking.

Luzia, unable to hold back her tears she wanted to be home quickly and climbed the stairs in four strides. She locked herself in her room, unable to speak a word. Her mother thought that it was one of those typical quarrels among friends and that everything would be OK the next day. But the next day and the following day, even after the festival was over, neither Esteban nor Luzia approached her. She did not receive any messages from Esteban either. Before, when he returned from the sea and did not have a chance to meet with Luzia, he would send his little brother to let her know what time they should go out. But all these days Esteban's brother never came.

The situation worried Mikela, Luzia's mother, and she thought she had to do something about it. As soon as the town festivals ended and the men went off to sea, she went to Karmen's house looking for an explanation. Karmen was not at home and Mikela thought it was probably better that way.

"Mikela, how come are you here this early? What's the matter?"

"Listen, Josepa, I'm not sure if you know this, but my daughter, Luzia, spent every single day of the town festivities at home because her friends turned their backs on her. Your daughter Karmen even told her to find new friends without giving her an explanation. I'm very hurt to see an old friend of my daughter acting like this. You don't do that to a childhood friend. I am here hoping you'll know something and will shed some light on this situation."

"Look, I don't know anything. Nothing."

"But you're Karmen's mother. She must've mentioned something."

"Well if you insist, I'll tell you. Truly, I'm angry with you myself because you haven't told me anything about what happened to Luzia. We've been like sisters for many years, our daughters have been friends from the day they were born, and honestly, I never thought you trusted me so little. Never. When Karmen told me what happened, I was furious but I didn't tell you anything."

"Josepa, I don't know what to say. What happened? Please, tell me."

"That . . . Luzia miscarried recently."

"What? Do you know what you're saying? Do you realize the seriousness of what you're saying? That she miscarried? Where did you get that information? Do you realize how repugnant what you're saying is?"

Even though Mikela was furious, she began crying. However, she did not want to leave that house without more information.

"I don't think you know what you're saying. You cannot make up something like this. A person's honor should not be destroyed based on a gossip sprung from a lie."

"You say I don't know what I'm talking about? You know what I'm talking about. You and your daughter know well what I'm saying. You both tried to trap Esteban without any consideration for my daughter. You must know whose is the miscarried baby. You have deceived poor Esteban. Now you two are on your own, the whole town knows about it."

Josepa poured onto Mikela all her fury, years of envy and jealousy. Mikela, sobbing like Mary Magdalene, left the house with a lump in her throat, which hardly allowed her to breathe. When she arrived home, she explained to Luzia what happened; they embraced and cried together for hours.

Luzia continued going to work but her relationship with her co-workers was no longer the same. Some looked down on her and she preferred to ignore the rest. Soon she was always alone and if by chance that were not the case, she would choose not to speak with anyone for hours. Her life was reduced to going back and forth from home to work and from work to home. She looked more listless by the day and began losing weight due to her lack of appetite. She grew paler and thinner.

One day, at work, she heard the conversation of a group of women working next to her. They did not regard Luzia in any way and, intending that she hear, said:

"Have you heard that Karmen is dating Esteban?"

"Now that you say it! I wasn't sure but I saw them the other day coming out of the cinema and Esteban had his arm around Karmen. It's great, isn't it? It was meant to be."

"Yes, they make a great couple. I'm happy to see decent, young people get together."

"I heard that they're getting married soon. They have it all, really."

"Yes, they're old enough and Esteban must have enough money saved by now. They have it made."

"I wish them happiness. They sure deserve it."

Luzia listened without lifting her head, without making the slightest gesture. And though those women expected her to do or say something, she proved them wrong. It was obvious that although they tried to provoke her, they did not get any reaction from Luzia, not a word, not a complaint, not even an insult. She kept working in silence.

And that is how the months went by, Luzia feeling sadder, weaker and paler by the day. Her mother, afraid Luzia had contracted some serious disease, took her to be seen by the best doctors in the adjoining city. When someone is sick in the family, one somehow finds money even where there is none. But doctors concluded that Luzia was not physically ill. They all agreed that Luzia presented another type of ailment, she had the worst of illnesses: lack of willingness to live.

They had a harsh winter that year and did not have a good fishing season. As a result of the lack of work, Luzia spent all winter secluded at home. On Sunday mornings all she did was attend the first mass early in the day to avoid being seen by the town's people. Besides that, she did not go anywhere.

Spring came and she began working. But Luzia was no longer the same cheerful, pleasant looking, young woman she was the year before. She resembled a forty-plus-year-old sickly woman. Mother asked her time after time to stay home, not to go to work, but Luzia did not listen. And that is how, one day in June, she heard at work through the grapevine, since she no longer had any friends left, that Karmen was to be married the following Sunday. No one was able to tell how Luzia felt when she learned the news. She stayed on task as if nothing were the matter.

But, by pure coincidence or because a Higher power wanted it, Luzia died the very same day Karmen was to get married. At dawn, quietly, the twenty-two-year-old woman left this world. It was almost nine on the day Luzia died that Karmen was to get married. Not only Luzia's neighbors but the whole town was aware of what was going on. Karmen was about to get married at nine and when the time came, the bride and groom, family members, and friends went to the church.

In those days, people got married in the church closest to their house and they all would walk there. They had to pass in front of Luzia's house to get to the church. When they passed by Luzia's house, her mother came out to the balcony and, consumed in sorrow, began cursing them.

"You've killed my daughter and from now on, may the rest of your days be damned. You will need to pay dearly for what you have done to my daughter. You'll suffer this curse for three generations. There won't be a legacy for this family; all will die. Esteban, fish will eat your eyes. Your children will disappear one after the other and you, Josepa, you will live to witness it all."

"Get back in the house, crazy woman! Those are nothing but the words of a lunatic!"

"The words of a lunatic that will come true!"

She shut the door as she was saying those last words. Caught by surprise those in the procession stopped in their tracks but quickly resumed walking.

Three or four years passed and Mikela died shortly after Luzia and Luzia's father went to live with one of his sisters. The house was empty.

After their marriage, Karmen and her husband went to live with Karmen's parents. And that is where she gave birth to her first and only child, a daughter. Though Luzia's house was empty, Karmen didn't like to pass it. She hid an overwhelming remorse and although she did not share her feelings with Esteban, she could not forget the curse Mikela inflicted on them and their offspring. She became obsessed;

she pictured Esteban's body torn to pieces. Although she did not tell her mother a word about her fears her mother began sensing her daughter's distress. She took to blessing their house with holy water she got from different churches, and lit candles as offerings to all the saints. She went daily to some church to beg for her family's good health. She did not have the slightest doubt that what Karmen said about Luzia's miscarriage was true; not the slightest doubt.

On the other hand, Karmen felt guiltier each day, and she thought of moving to another house. Esteban pointed out all the inconveniences that came with moving out of her parents' home but she ended up getting her way. However, she did not get the peace of mind she hoped for. Though they changed houses, the guilt continued to bother her. And what's more, the fright and restlessness grew, especially when Esteban was gone to sea and she found herself alone in the house. Those days were very hard. Once, when she was asleep, she woke up thinking she had heard someone knocking on the door. She got up and when she opened the door, she realized there was no one there but as soon as she went back to bed, she heard the knocking once again, this time coming from the balcony. She got up and, shivering in fear, tiptoed to the balcony wondering whom she would find there. But she did not see anyone. Another time while she was in the kitchen, she suddenly heard someone forcefully shutting the windows. Then she heard the doorknocker. On windless days, doors kept swinging back and forth. Karmen was overcome by fear. The most normal things frightened her. Finally, she told her mother how she was feeling. But she did not share the likely source of her fear because Karmen believed all this could be part of Luzia's retaliation. Her mother suggested she go to talk to a priest, thinking that his counsel could be helpful. Following her mother's advice, she went to see a priest. She did not share with him what she had done to Luzia. She just told him that they had a few disagreements.

"Listen," said the priest, "it looks like Luzia doesn't feel at peace where she is, maybe because of what you told me. So, it would be best if you went to her to ask for forgiveness. Therefore, go to her gravesite and ask her to forgive you. You must do this soon so your soul can rest." And as he said these last words, he blessed her.

Following the priest's advice, the next morning, at the magical time of daybreak, Karmen went to the cemetery. She knew where Luzia's gravesite was because she had been there before. The humble cross was located between two big mausoleums and she directed her steps that way. When she arrived, she saw someone sitting on one of the mausoleums. She ignored the person, thinking that it was the mausoleum owner or a family member of the deceased who was buried there. She thought that she would need to wait until the person left so she sat at the grave closest to her. A few minutes had past when she heard someone calling her name. The person calling her was the woman sitting on the mausoleum. She could not see her face clearly because it was covered with a shawl, but she was sure she did not know her. It was not easy to see if she were young or old. She heard her name again but this time she thought the voice sounded somewhat familiar.

"Karmen, come closer, do not be afraid, come closer!"

Not so much scared this time as surprised, Karmen approached. Her initial surprise turned into fear. The woman sitting there was Luzia.

"Are you frightened? You should be. You can't hold the burden you're carrying in your heart. That burden is what has brought you to me."

"Forgive me, Luzia! For my daughter's love. Forgive me! I know the pain that I caused you but I wanted Esteban for myself."

"Do you see the tin can next to the big bucket full of water? Fill it up and bring it to me. Do as I say."

Karmen did what Luzia asked her and brought her the can filled with water.

"Spill the water on this gravestone's marble top."

Karmen spilled the water.

"Now, go ahead and gather it up again," asked Luzia.

"I can't. You know that's impossible," said Karmen.

"What I know is that you tarnished my honor and reputation in front of everyone in town and that you condemned me to misfortune. And in the same way that spilled water cannot be re-gathered, one cannot build up her good name once it has been disgraced."

And as she said these last words, Luzia vanished. Karmen, then, crazed, adrift, unaware of where her footsteps were taking her, left the cemetery. About noon, when they realized she had not returned home, they began searching for her. At dusk, on top of Tonpoi Handi near the cemetery, they found her slippers and, down from there, amid the rocks, her cardigan.

IRATI ELORRIETA

Bilbao, 1979

*W*hile Irati Elorrieta was a university student, she traveled to Berlin and has made her home there. *Burbuilak* (Bubbles, 2008), her only novel so far, and all her short stories written since then, have sprung from two sources of inspiration, Bilbao and Berlin.

Her novel was published first in Basque and then Spanish and was well received. A compilation of lyric short stories that all revolve around characters who end up in Berlin. Stories that talk about loneliness like the one found in this collection.

She has also translated into Basque Daniel Glattauer's *Gut gegen Nordwind* (2006) as *Ipar haizearen kontra* (2012).

Torn Landscapes

When they erected the wind turbines in our valley, time split in two. My lifetime also splits before and after Iris, because everything changed with Iris.

I first saw Iris at Claude and Yumiko's wedding. I quietly observed her from a distance, with the same prudence and fascination Father taught me was needed to observe rare birds. Claude and Yumiko celebrated their wedding at the end of autumn, when the first geese and crane flocks cross the sky on the way south. I did not see Iris again until the beginning of the following spring. On that second occasion, we traveled from Berlin to Bellin sitting next to each other. And so our journey began with the two hours it took us to transform the *r* into an *l*, at about the same time the cranes return to their mating grounds. Destiny was toying with us.

There are a few meters separating us, but Iris is inside and I am outside. I am sitting in my Ford Fiesta, watching Iris in her house, right in front of me, standing in front of the window of the room she uses as her workplace. Right when I turn off the headlights, Iris goes back into her workroom and switches on the desk lamp. Though the window is open, the rolling of the thunder prevents her from hearing the car's engine turn off. She looks for her pack of cigarettes in the drawer, pulls one out with her long fingernails, puts it to her lips, and lights it with a match. Lately she paints her nails in a dark-red shade. After dinner, once she has taken the children to bed, Iris smokes a cigarette in her workroom. She does not smoke in the other rooms of the house. But she does in the workroom, with the windows open. Even with today's downpour, she smokes a cigarette in front of the open window. She holds the cigarette in one hand bracing her arm with her other hand. Skilled hands that have been working with leather all day. She's looking at the pieces lain out on her worktable, who knows what she is thinking. I would enter her workroom quietly while she is immersed in her thoughts. I would stand behind her and carefully approach to smell the nape of her neck. I would like to go one by one through the different layers of scents that have stuck to her skin through the course of the day. And while at it, I would place my hands on her thighs clad in tight jeans and with my eyes closed would inhale deeper to reach the core of her scents. I would slide my hands down her thighs. Iris has muscular legs; thighs whose strong muscles oscillate when she walks in high heels. Those thighs, the starting points of her long legs, which taper into her high-heeled shoes. Those thighs that oscillate when she walks in high heels, I would gently pull toward my body.

After stubbing out the cigarette, Iris goes to shut the window and before she could see me sitting in the car, I flash the headlights to announce my presence. Perhaps she might have not recognized me anyway, but I want to avoid any misunderstanding. I would not like for Iris to think that I secretly spy on her. I stay in the car so I will not disturb her after-dinner cigarette ritual. But Iris would never believe an explanation like that. She would not believe that I have waited respectfully for her to extinguish her cigarette in the ashtray and walk up to shut the window.

I have startled her for a minute and blinded her with the headlights. When she regains her sight, I wave at her from inside the car. I make a gesture with my hand to reassure her it's me so I don't frighten her, but I feel ridiculous waving my hand and I let the movement die out. I point outside of the window with my finger, "Look at how it's pouring." I shake the same finger in a negative motion and then make a gesture with my hand as if I were holding an umbrella. I am sure that she is thinking I'm a fool. I always have the feeling that Iris looks at me like people look at little children.

I could get out of the car and take five or six steps to reach the entrance of the building. She will be wondering why I am making such a fuss about the rain. But I'd prefer her to think I'm a fool rather than to think I have been spying on her. She leaves her workroom and I don't see her for a few seconds. I remember her smell after getting out of the water. Wrapped in the brown blanket that I keep in my car, she snuggled against me looking for warmth. She let her wet hair down and rested her head on my shoulder. A scattered lightning flash. The light in the entryway comes on, and once more Iris surfaces. She walks up to the car sheltered under a gray umbrella with red polka dots, with the soft swing of her thighs that I fondly recalled earlier. I roll down the window and let her know that I forgot my iPod in the house. She asks me if I know where I left it. I answer that I left it in the girls' room when Naomi asked me to go up to see the little lamp they made in daycare. The continuous tapping of the rain on the roof. "The girls are asleep," answers Iris, as if she were telling me something I did not already know. Iris is patient under the rainstorm. "I know they are asleep," I tell her, "but I know that I left my iPod on the yellow nightstand." "And you want to come up now?" She always has to show her superiority in every unimportant matter. Although the tips of her shoes are getting wet with the splashing raindrops that furiously explode against the ground, she cannot overlook that I'm here at such an inopportune time. "Yes, I want to come up now," I tell her, "to bother you," I think, "I came here with that sole purpose."

Iris has made clear to me more than once that she does not like to have me come to her house more often than necessary. If I surpass the occasions she determines necessary, she walks up to me, places her hand on her hip and looks at me like one looks at a dog. Yes, when she wants to throw me out of her house, Iris makes me feel like a dog. Nevertheless, I continue doing whatever I'm doing at that moment, as long as she does not say anything. If I'm in the shower, I keep showering. If I'm reading my e-mails, I answer as many messages I can until Iris, without uttering a word, pushes the button and the screen turns black.

Steps toward the building entrance, next to her, under the umbrella. Iris walks next to me, very close to me. But still, I'm not able to smell the aroma her body emanates because her cold demeanor makes me tense. The sound of her high heels' tapping echoes Iris' firmness.

Iris treats me as if I were some repairperson who has come to her house a couple of times on service calls. This behavior is out-of-place, keeping in mind that I come to her house two or three times a week to bring our daughters back from daycare.

Naomi and Selene share the same bed. Selene's closed fists show their readiness to fight even while she is asleep. Naomi is a little older and Selene feels like she must always defend herself. She tries to catch up with her sister in an effort to erase their age difference. Naomi is breathing through her mouth because she has nasal congestion. It seems to me that Naomi reacts in complete calmness to her sister's struggle to be older. She lets her be so she can believe for a little while that she has achieved her goal. But soon after, *zast*, she regains her advantage with little effort.

Iris is standing at the door of the girls' room, her right hand on her hip. I'm sitting on Selene's bedside and show Iris the iPod but I do not stand up. I stamp a kiss on each girl's cheek and pull up the covers. Do you have to react like that, Iris, just because I took a minute to watch my daughters while they sleep? I wish you would soften up a little and offer me a truce. As I'm walking by her I think of kissing her too to soften her shell with a gentle gesture. She would think I was drunk.

For once, car cigarette lighters become useful, and together with the adaptor to connect the iPod, I have all the music I need in my Ford Fiesta. Father used to listen to cassettes in this car. "Andoni," he would tell me when I was riding along with him, "Will you transfer these CDs to cassettes so I can play them in the car?" I have a hard time understanding why Father drove a car with a cassette deck when he did not have any financial difficulties and was not stingy. I still drive Father's Ford Fiesta, not for nostalgic reasons but because I can't afford anything else. I am not nostalgic. When I inherited Father's car, before I returned to Berlin, I threw all the cassette-filled boxes he had in his trunk into the dump.

I drive while listening to opera with the storm's soundtrack as background music. Catalani's first act, *La Wally*. It happens to be the bootlegged recording of the aria secretly made by the postman character in the film *Diva*. There is no one in the streets. The storm and the rain fill the deserted space. The headlights pierce the storm, opening the way for me. The downpour turns into high heels tapping on my head. The telephone rings. I wonder if it's Iris asking me to keep her company because she feels lonely. Will she ever have such a moment of insomnia? The cat's meow ring-tone belongs to Elisa's phone. She is calling me to check that I'm headed to the *Kontainer* in my car. As if she didn't know that I don't use the Metro! She asks me if I wouldn't mind picking her up, if I'm still on the road. I'm about to tell her I can't because I would need to retrace a section of the road I've already driven. But I'm enjoying listening to the opera so I tell her to expect me in ten minutes.

Sometimes I wonder if Iris really wants to see me leave when she shows me to the door. On those occasions, I prolong my stay by continuing to read the newspaper while stealing a few last sips of coffee. Iris, don't you think that the kitchen and the living room feel too empty when I leave? What do you do under the silence of your sheets after you rush me off?

In the car, along with the opera, Elisa and I enter a time and space capsule. The rain reinforces the impression, as the city in the distance appears fogged. The raindrops that plunge down the windshield soak the few city lights making them seem bigger.

"May I turn off the music, Andoni?" pleads Elisa with her finger already on the dial.

We are quiet and the opera is overtaken by the sound of the motor, the tires running on the asphalt, and the tapping of the rain. We cross paths with a speeding ambulance whose siren outdoes the storm.

"Ambulances unsettle me," confesses Elisa and she trembles, "They put me on alert mode for a few seconds. You too?"

"The siren's wailing is penetrating, yes, it stirs up a basic desire to be at peace," I agree with her. I confess something else to her too. "Sometimes I imagine that I'm the person waiting for the ambulance."

"Does that thought arouse you?" she teases me.

"It's nothing macabre, just a moment of empathy, which dissipates as soon as the sound of the siren muffles in the distance."

The November downpour wants to consume us. On our way from the car to the *Kontainer* Elisa holds my arm and I like the way she touches me. We are soaking wet as we go in. I take my jacket off and help her get hers off, then I hang both in the beverage storage room. Elisa takes a seat on the sofa with Niall, Sho, and the others. She invites me to join them but I don't feel like it and even though I don't have a shift today, I go behind the counter among the glasses filled with red wine. I would prefer to get a taste of Iris's favorite but wine also helps me warm up.

I do not mention Iris in my conversations with Elisa or the others. Consequently, Iris is increasingly adopting the status of a character in my mind. And when she is in front of me, I feel out of place, as if they ordered me to land in a world that I have imagined. Plus, the elements in that world are familiar to me but they don't behave as I want them to.

Today, for example, we got caught in the rainstorm, and when we made it home, I let Naomi and Selene play in the puddles in the courtyard until they got tired. Iris was working, as usual, with the radio on. She loves listening to books read aloud on the radio and she becomes restless if we get in her way. I convinced them to change their clothes from head to toe and dry their hair in exchange for what they call "*children's coffee.*" I brewed some real coffee too and I entered Iris's workroom to offer her a cup. Her sewing machine and

radio were going at the same time, *treek-trak, treek-trak*. I
left her coffee on the table. *Suddenly, without knowing why,
Prince Andrew got nervous.* I asked her what she was listening
to. "Tolstoi," she replied dryly without lifting an eye from her
stitching. Where did she hide her vulnerable and nicer tones
of voice? I am used to talking to Iris without speaking. Her
world is impenetrable. *What does she think about? Why is she
happy? Prince Andrew wondered full of curiosity and against
his own will.* I remained gazing at her in silence. I substituted
Iris's voice for that of the narrator on the radio, and her voice
enveloped me, as if she would surround me with her arms.
Her hands, which so skillfully handle leather, also happen to
be very crafty when moving across my body. I feel naked. I
lose my head between her thighs, down in her forest and I
don't feel like leaving. Iris lifts her eyes, sips her coffee, and
suddenly an Iris that is not the one who inhabits my thoughts
confronts me. I'm not in control of the situation. Iris could
easily erase my existence. She doesn't need me in her world.
I see it; if I don't leave her workroom, she's going to attack
me with her rough scowls. But I don't leave. I inhale deeply
and close my eyes to listen to the murmur of the radio. When
I was a child, every weekend when I woke up, I would hear
the sounds of the radio coming from the first floor. Mother
always had the radio on. To this day I connect the sound of
the radio with Mother's presence. It's so soothing.

Elisa asks me to serve her a beer. She likes men who are
ready to give up something just to please her whims. Niall
gave up Anette as result of the affair he had with Elisa. That
is one of the versions, anyway, because Niall is no fool. At
Claude and Yumiko's wedding, while all the guests gathered
in the attic to listen to Sho's solo performance, Niall disappeared with Elisa. But I would swear that by then Anette al-

ready had a foot out the door. When they went up to the roof holding hands, they didn't realize I was there too and I witnessed their intimacy in silence. Elisa might think that Niall succumbed to her seductive powers. But it's possible that Niall had already suspected that Annette was about to leave him and wanted to begin consoling himself before he felt the heartbreak. All stories have, at least, two versions.

Elisa's concert begins with an air of a psychological journey. Her compositions are full of everyday sounds, but with unusual combinations created by chance. Once again, she opens a way toward a dream world for me.

Elisa is a complete diva and each conquest she makes pleases her. Still, she acts without malice. She is nothing but a romantic. Since princes are hard to find, she sleeps with men who are a long ways from being princes, including those who are not available. And of those who are, she finds the oddest ones, for example, a coworker from the radio station who she used to bring to the *Kontainer.*

I agree with Elisa when she says that one should not have prejudices. She says that having prejudices is missing opportunities. But I feel satisfied just watching intently. I learned to observe intently when I took long walks with Father. In the forest, if we walked stealthily on fallen leaves, we could watch jays, cuckoos, and turtledoves. In grain fields or amid dense undergrowth, whitethroats and playful yellowhammers. Father trained me to distinguish white sparrow hawks and marsh hawks, red kites and black kites, big owls and medium-sized owls and large hawks and wasp-eating ones, all from a distance. He taught me that it was helpful to face the wind when observing birds to avoid giving away your presence. That way we are very different. Elisa prefers to gather physical evidence, from flesh. When I first saw Iris, I ate her up with my eyes. Without touching her, I knew that I would feel the desire to be with her for a long time.

Elisa's lyrics come packed with memories. At first they come across as playful but unexpectedly they become menacing under the surface. Elisa knows that dreams have dark sides. The loud voices of a group of children playing on the street turn into the squawking of a flock of ducks. What at first was a delightful melody turns annoying. In winter, flocks of skylarks cross the plains of Orbaibar. This bird imitates the songs of other birds. Mother stayed right there after Father died, managing alone, as if she were a local, becoming a native. Mother understands well the impossibility of my return to my hometown but I still feel that I'm to blame and escape, flying away with the screeching of notes too high to reach. Migratory animals can lose their direction. Iris blames me for the situation. I guess I always show up at the wrong times. I have put off visiting Mother for too long because I cannot show up there without Naomi and Selene.

The voices become distorted, appearing and disappearing between dog barks and machine noises, like when losing a radio signal. Elisa plays with different sounds, they entangle, with no regard for others. It is Elisa's gift, to bring together into one body threads of disparate origins. That body is a cloud, a state of consciousness. A room where there is space for everything.

I keep telling Iris that, even though we are separated, we could try having a better relationship. If nothing else, for the girls. What am I supposed to tell Naomi when she asks me why I don't stay for dinner? Or when she says she wants to come to my place? One day I tell her that I can't, that I'm busy. But if I keep telling her the same thing, she will believe it's nothing but an excuse. And what am I supposed to tell her, "Your mom doesn't want me to stay for dinner?" Then Naomi will ask her mom why doesn't she want me there. What are you going to tell her then, Iris? That you are afraid to give in to what your body yearns for? Truly, Iris's defensive behavior doesn't help. Besides, she does it to make me feel bad, to emphasize that I'm not good enough for our daughters. Iris needs to feel superior to me. She needs to make me feel insignificant.

Claude and Yumiko are looking for a place to sit. Yumiko is already showing. I have not shared this with Claude but I have noticed that she ignores me ever since Iris handed me the list of rules. I walked up to them and when I was pouring some wine in Claude's glass, I whispered in his ear, "Are you sure the baby is yours?"

Rules, Iris says. Well, I don't need any rules. One of these days I'm going to run out of patience, I'll pick Naomi and Selene up from daycare, put them in the Ford Fiesta and the three of us will drive all the way to Mother's so we can take a vacation from rules. Because after all, my mother has the right to spend time with her own grandchildren. We will have homemade blackberry jam for breakfast. Naomi, Selene, and I will hold hands while going for walks and pick rosemary, thyme, and lavender. We'll kneel to watch small lizards resting in the sun. I'll take them up to Gerinda Park and we'll echo the buzzing of the wind turbines screaming our lungs out. Then I'll bring them back. But in the meantime, I'll teach Iris a lesson. So she realizes that I have my say in this too and that even though she systematically silences me, ignores me, and belittles me, I'll show her that I can get back at her. Later, I'll take her to the bedroom and remind her what it's like to feel intensely.

I must be one of the few in our group of friends who

has not slept with Elisa but when I listen to her music, I immerse myself in her mental space full of memories and fantasies. I get into her head as she gets into mine. She activates emotions in me that have been turned off during the day. Through a tunnel, at the speed necessary to reach the summit. Cacophonies of fear, joy, sadness, peace, order, and chaos.

I first noticed Iris at Claude and Yumiko's wedding. An aerial view, from the rooftop. The same rooftop from which, for many years, Claude, Niall, and I transmitted our independent radio programming. She arrived along with the sunset, when sparrows began filling the sky with black dots before landing on construction cranes. She arrived by bicycle, her high heels on the pedals, a long dress down to her ankles, with her back exposed. Sparrows are supposed to be bearers of happiness but there is always a bearer of news who enjoys pulling your leg. I assumed she was one of Yumiko's friends since I had never seen her with Claude. She took her sunglasses off to kiss Claude and Yumiko, her fingernails covered with gray polish, and her blond hair gathered in a bun. The confident sureness of her movement dazzled me. She did everything with precision, making it seem indispensable. How she brushed her hair from her face, how she took a cigarette from the pack Claude offered her, how she lifted her foot to scratch her ankle. Apparently, she must have known the other guests since she seemed to be at ease drifting from group to group. Unless someone had been watching her closely, no one would have noticed how many times she filled her glass with white wine. Her dress clung to her like a second skin on her breast and waist, slipping down her thighs all the way to her ankles. Her feet paused on the floor yet she walked on her toes, as if ready to fly away at any moment. Elusive.

I found out that Claude had met her when he worked at the call center. She had begun drinking too much after losing her job and that, encouraged by the job-center, she was looking to further her professional formation. "She is looking for help to reorganize her life," said Claude.

I saw her put her empty glass down by the door before she slipped away. She left without saying goodbye to anyone. That day I did not talk with her but I tried to register as many details as I could. And with all the data I gathered, I was certain: she had the power to generate wind and her murmuring would generate a shivering within me from which I would lose my center.

Noise Music has taught me that there are different ways to listen to sound. It depends on each person. Everything is up for interpretation. Once when I was a child, I heard screams in the middle of the night. I thought it must have been a child lost in the forest and I got up, looked out the window and, since I didn't see anything, rushed to wake up my parents. Father told me it was a fox. But I kept hearing the child lost in the forest asking for help. That same afternoon before I left the house to go to the forest with a neighborhood friend to pick chamomile and mushrooms, Father warned me not to stray from the path, that we could become captives of thorny box trees. And instead of a fox, I heard the child who had strayed away from the path, unable to get out of the thick bramble of the forest.

I have always feared places with no exits. That is the reason why the abandoned mines of Erreniega or the Beriain reservoir quicksand have a mythlike status for me. I used to picture both sites full of dead bodies. Cities, on the other hand, have exits. I took Iris out of the *Kontainer* and Berlin when I felt the monotony of the day was about to swallow her.

It had been Claude's idea and mine to organize a concert in support of the Irtijal Festival in Lebanon. We organized fundraising concerts at the *Kontainer.* We brought musicians now settled in Europe who were originally from Arabic countries, together with local ones. Claude jammed with a trumpet player from Jerusalem. The string of short, experimental music performances put a nice tone to the night. A huge crowd attended and, until the wee hours of the morning, apparently drank to the health of those who wanted to raise a space for music free from the detritus of war. That night, the morning did not catch me at the *Kontainer.*

It was a weekend in April. I had gone to the train station to pick up one of the musicians who had been delayed. I was parking my car in front of the *Kontainer* when I saw Iris arrive on her bicycle. She had pulled up the collar of her pea coat. Her jacket was yellow and she wore tight jeans that ended at her high-heeled shoes, which lifted her from the ground. I noticed that the gaze of the saxophone player sitting next to me followed her all the way to the door.

It had been easy to spot Iris in her yellow pea coat while everyone else was dressed in black. I watched her intently so it would be obvious that I was looking at her. With that look I promised myself Iris would not return home on her bicycle.

That night I did not beat around the bush in my attempts to get close to Iris. While she was chatting with Claude, I approached them with complete ease. When Claude left I did not leave my post. Iris, though not lowering her guard, accepted my company. I was alert, waiting for the right moment when her suspicion would be disarmed and I could offer her something to get her to come closer to me.

When she told me, "Do you know what I want?" I knew that was my chance. I was ready to give her anything she asked for.

"I want the ocean," she said.

"What would you do with the ocean?"

"I would get in the water."

"I'll take you," I said. She smiled. I stood up and grabbed her yellow coat. "We'll be there in two hours."

"Are you serious? How are we going to go to the ocean now?"

"How? By car."

At midnight we left the city headed north. Together, on the run, crossing the darkness sprinkled with the red lights of the wind farms. "The driving distance from my town to the ocean is also two hours. An hour and a half to Donostia and about two hours to Hendaia. There too, the landscape is full of wind turbines. Mighty giants, whose visual impact, the torn up landscape and memories, the death of birds and bats spark debate. But there is no doubt that they appear imposing standing up against the sky." We drove across the wind territory on our way to the ocean. The red lights shimmered in the dark of the night yet the towers and propellers could not be seen. A constellation of red lights. Iris asked me:

"So the landscape back home looks like this?"

I told her that the landscape back home looked like her. That it consisted of two types of topography, mountainous and flat lands.

"The only thing that the landscape outside the city and my homeland have in common is the wind turbines. This is flat terrain. There, on the other hand, the turbines have been erected in rows along the mountain ridges. There is hardly a mountaintop without a turbine, except the area near Olleta."

Iris folds her legs to the side while on the seat and her high heels dig lightly into my jeans. She listened to my account with her eyes half-closed.

"Olleta happens to be the hometown of a very well-known film director. The town is located at the base of a mountain. That's the kind of small town that's found in our valley, formed by clusters of houses.

"How famous is that director?"

"He almost won an Oscar once."

"What do you mean, almost?

"Yes, almost."

"Almost isn't winning."

I used to ride my bike along the mountain paths and listen to the owl calls and observe the sparring of the birds of prey. I reiterated to her that the landscape of my homeland resembled her. That it consisted of two types of topography, mountainous and flats. Thick forests and plowed land.

"And which do you like better?"

"You," I told her.

"No. The forest or the flat lands?"

"They can't be separated."

They cannot be separated because they are threads that intertwine. Where one ends, the other begins. Box trees and junipers spread on the flatlands as they wish. Rows of vines and almond trees merge into umber colored plowed fields. And the narrow paths edged with the light-yellowish color of the canola plants trace curves on the fields. Behind the hill, a cluster of houses, a small town. Above the town there is a small hill covered with forests. Straight and curved lines. Order and chaos.

"I don't see the similarity between that landscape of yours and me."

"In Springtime patches of yellow like your jacket appear in the fields in the flatlands."

Among the heather, gorse flowers bring life to a landscape dried by the sun and the wind.

"And what are you doing here, so far from there?"

"Taking you to the ocean."

We kept driving in silence for a while, hidden in an undetermined nowhere of the freeway. I drove the next kilometers longing for the landscape of my youth. With the melancholy of one who remembers from far away, with my skin transformed into a feeling. And the longing for my birth land mixed in my veins with the desire I felt for Iris.

"Is this it?" She asked when I turned off the car.

"In the city one forgets that the ocean is close."

It is not close, but it is at such a distance that one can take the car and come when one feels the urge. It is necessary to cross the forest to get to Bellin's beach. The beach is on a bay and a large tract of land embraced us when we arrived.

"Aren't you going to get in the water?" she asked me.

"No, not me. I'll wait here for you."

I gave her the blanket I had in the trunk and we walked toward the seashore. Reeds edged the shore. She dropped the blanket on the sand and got undressed. I saw her get into the water.

When she came out, she covered herself with the blanket and picked up her clothes. She walked up to me. She sat next to me and rested her head on my shoulder. I hugged her through the blanket. I felt her body warming up against mine.

I slipped my hand through Iris's wet hair, stopping behind the fold of her ear, then continued down her neck and caressed her wet skin. With my fingertips I filled her skin with pathways, making each path of the new territory mine and drying the droplets in the row between her breasts. When I surrounded both breasts, I stumbled upon the white of their peaks. I hid my head under the blanket and licked her nipples and discovered new territories along her body. I repeatedly caressed her waist and thighs. I advanced from her belly down across her pubic hair driven by the desire to reach her vagina's moist mouth. When I introduced my finger into her warm vagina, Iris was laying down, her body completely stretched on the sand. I felt at home inside Iris, as I hadn't felt for a long time.

There is nothing like waking up to the sound of the waves and rustling leaves at the break of dawn. The whispering of the ocean penetrated us. The first rays of light and the loud trumpet-like sounds of the cranes flying above our heads foretold longer and sunnier days to come. The crane flocks predict a fertile season, but apparently, they also predict quarrels.

With the first signs of the night, the *Kontainer* turns into dense darkness. It makes you not want to move from there, to find yourself a cozy corner in such a hideout and join whoever happens to be next to you. I can hardly see Elisa and the others amid the smoke. If their lively murmuring would not had given them away I would have thought they were gone. I take a sip from the little wine left in the bottle and without grabbing my jacket, I go out to breathe some fresh air. I walk through the door and I feel as if someone had emptied a bucket of water on my head. I look up but I don't see anyone to harass.

I turn the heat all the way up in the Ford Fiesta, but it is useless since it does not work. In order to feel my body's shivering a little bit less, I turn the music up. I have all kinds of music on my iPod and destiny plays *Dire Straits*. This is the music of my parent's car when we went on vacation. "I do the Walk, I do the Walk of Life . . ." What the heck. I turn off the iPod and I curse my wet clothes. I curse the storm's tireless tenacity. "Tell me the name of the damned one that has led you from the path." It's hard to know. No one knows if the storm has separated the lost bird or if it has suffered a malfunction in its internal navigation system. It is not easy to understand the reason.

Our valley was about to disappear. Forgotten, away from the road until the mighty giants were sown on the hills. Right where the mountains and the sky separate, they erected towers one hundred meters high, white tree forests.

Forgotten yet full of memories. The traces of time remain in the bent oak branches and cavities of the rocks. Foreign bodies on this map of memories, they might become part of the landscape or do they tear it with the tension they spark? Like the electric fork of lightning tears the sky.

There is no shortage of damned targets to curse. Power companies that make money installing propellers in the paths of birds and bats. Long power lines that electrocute and kill. We can also curse the hunters who wait on the roads. And of course, the cars that run over and kill more than one bird. After all, don't bats choose to approach those seductive structures that end up shattering their lungs?

I could curse Iris; I could curse Claude. But the first one to be damned is and will always be fate. Because fate is the inevitable path, there is nothing else; it is the only sure thing. Anything can happen along the way and we do not know if we win more than we lose.

If Iris tried to connect Andoni to something positive, she would draw a blank. She could think of Andoni's generosity, of the level head he shows when faced with certain situations, of the stories he can tell so sweetly, of the curiosity his knowledge of animal peculiarities shows. For Iris all that became worthless almost from the start and it is not easy for her to think of anything that she would categorize as a happy experience. Still, if she makes an effort to go back to the source of everything, she feels a tickle coming all the way from her vagina to her stomach and she feels the need to contract her inner muscles. But that is not something she would share with Naomi and Selene if they were ever to begin asking questions.

Now, while the girls are asleep and she is in her workroom looking at the pieces of leather scattered on the table, she would say in retrospect that everything happened fast. At first, she felt trapped by the situation but changes came one after the other and by the time she realized, she had been able to bring her life to a new place. Things are going well for Iris now. She handed Andoni a list of rules to follow, she set boundaries, and since then, her contact with him is as minimal as possible.

Before, she spent her time waiting for Andoni. It was not just about the time she had wasted; if that weren't enough, that wasted time, already rotten, began rotting her disposition too.

It is very different though to wait for Alex. It is a kind of waiting that will bring happiness and, while it gets prolonged, the appetite for the pleasure that is about to come increases. Today, because of the storm, he will come by car. He has a deadline this week so he let her know that he will come quite late. Iris opens a bottle of wine and puts the last touches on the piece she has almost finished while enjoying her body's slowly building arousal. With her second glass she leaves the day behind, and the night will be for what she wants. Now it is Alex that she wants.

When she met Andoni, days did not seem to have a set

beginning or end, any time was good to have sex. When he finished his shift at the *Kontainer*, he would go home and would look for Iris's complicity with his most erect body appendage. Or when Iris fell asleep curled up fitting his body, before they got up, he would get on top of her and provoke her with pleasurable tickles. Andoni often used to stay in bed until noon, and, if Iris was still home, wherever he found her, he took her in his arms first gently and later firmly. Whenever Andoni did not have to go to work, the nights would become endless. They would begin in the bathtub, continue with a bottle of Champagne or a gin and tonic. They would prolong their foreplay with no rush to consummate the act.

As soon as the sex fever wore out, Iris realized that she had to get rid of Andoni. She saw him as too generous, too natural, too sweet. He was generous with everyone and too spontaneous, you could not make plans with him because he needed to decide everything on the spot. Besides, his ideas were too romantic. He fell in love with the idea of falling in love with Iris. With Iris or, more precisely, with the idea of continuing to live inside Iris. He was missing a piece of reality until Iris confronted him with it: "Andoni we have to stop seeing each other." A very direct and clear statement, yet Andoni did not understand. Two days later, he was back at her doorstep, wishing Iris would forget about her decision. "Andoni, I don't want you to come anymore," she insisted. And Andoni gazed at her as if she were speaking a language he did not understand.

Iris realizes that the storm, instead of going away, is closer now. She hopes that the rolling of the thunder will not wake Naomi and Selene.

It had been a harsh irony to find out that, when she asked Andoni to get out of her life, she was pregnant with Naomi.

She decided to talk to Claude about her pregnancy before she talked with anyone else and he said something she did not expect:

"Wasn't that what you wanted?"

"To get pregnant with Andoni?"

"To have a reason to quit drinking and experience a change in your life. Here you have it, two birds with one stone."

Claude's words left her speechless. With time she came to agree with him: it had been the beginning of a new era. Motherhood, the chance to redirect her profession, a change of residence and the opportunity to begin working with her leather business as her own boss from home, and then, Alex. One after another. So if she had to say something positive about Andoni, it would have to be that he moved her life in a new direction with that stupid idea of going to the ocean.

Andoni has repeated to her incessantly, weren't they going to try at least? Iris never thought that just because Andoni and she had two daughters in common they would get along. Her parents had raised four daughters, and even though they could not stand each other, they stayed together because of the *children*. Iris, with a cynical face, begins keeping track: her oldest sister married for a second time, the second sister is divorced, and the third one is a lesbian. She fills her glass and drinks to her own health.

As a child she got the job of the messenger between her parents and they used her in their disputes. They made her do and say things against her will, to lie, for example. Iris was always ready to do anything so her parents would not fight. As a little girl, her parents' arguments really frightened her. As an adult she came to understand that her sisters and she were not the cause of their parents' arguments. But Cleo was the first one to stand her ground. Father kicked her out of the house when she introduced them to her girlfriend. The sequel was that Mother left the house with Iris.

When Naomi was born, Iris pleaded Andoni to fade from her life on his own. But, instead, there he was proclaiming the right to experience fatherhood. She half expected to see him with a ten-foot banner like the activists seeking self-determination, freedom from conformity, or the anti-Israeli protesters. He would come to see Naomi and stay for dinner, he would take a shower before leaving for work or, if he was off that night, he would sit down to watch TV. By the time she realized he was always there Andoni had turn into a squatter in her house.

She grabs a bottle of wine and remembers that other bottle of wine she bought to celebrate when she decided to stop breastfeeding Naomi. Naomi was six month old and Iris wanted to start training as a furrier through the Job Center. Andoni did not like the idea. But who asked for his opinion? Andoni came to see Naomi whenever it suited him. And Iris wanted to reclaim her body, her life, her plans, and her dreams.

That night, once again, Andoni was in her house. Iris was having dinner in the kitchen while he took Naomi to bed. She opened the bottle bought especially for the occasion and downed her first glass in one gulp. She felt the warmth within her body at once. She poured herself another glass and began drinking it in small sips this time. With each sip she felt a gust of wind straight to her head, a warm gust of wind that swept her thoughts away. Andoni walked into the kitchen and gazed at Iris's glass. "I am going to stop breastfeeding," Iris told him, "and I want to celebrate it with this bottle of wine." Andoni usually stayed for dinner, but that night she was the one who asked him if he wanted to stay to celebrate the milestone with her. She poured a glass for Andoni and they toasted. As the glass emptied, Iris's head was deactivating and her desire ignited. The party was on.

After a year-and-a-half drought, the wine irrigated her body and she overflowed with a desire to have sex. Andoni was in front of her eating dinner, both were laughing. The situation was unusual and it invited unusual things to the imagination. So, it was no coincidence for Iris's feet to entangle with Andoni's. Neither one stopped the game taking place under the table. They had sex in the kitchen and she came at once. The very same day Iris stopped breastfeeding, she got pregnant with Selene.

No matter what, Iris was not about to give Andoni the space he wanted. Andoni wanted to define the space he demanded: whenever he wanted it, whenever it suited him. And Iris instead, limited his space. Andoni would do anything for anyone. He was supportive of projects that were about to be shutdown, of people on the brink of being deported, of those who must pay for a lawyer so they can be defended before the persecution from the government. He would be willing to go at any time of the night to pick up a friend, load the car with someone's things, and bring him home. But he would not get out of bed on time to take Naomi to the doctor. Andoni does not get up in the morning because he spends the night drinking. On the contrary, no one checks with Iris to see if it will work for her. She does what needs to be done. That's all.

At first, she could not handle Andoni always being late or not showing up at all. It infuriated her having to change her plans because of Andoni's perpetual tardiness and unreliability. Iris was not willing to have to organize her day dependent on someone else. She soon stopped calling him when he did not show up and without waiting for him, she would go out with her daughters. If she stayed home, the girls could see Andoni out the window whenever he decided to show up. If they realized that Iris did not let him come into the house, she would be the mean parent. And she did not plan to be the mean one in this story.

Ever since she gave him her list of rules, Andoni picks the girls up twice a week from daycare and if he does not have too big of a hangover, he takes them for a few hours on Saturdays or Sundays. Iris is the one who decides who stays and who does not in her house. It is her house, her space. And Andoni does not need to be in a space that belongs to her, among her things, using her things. Boundaries. Iris has set boundaries and she does not permit Andoni to mix with anything that is hers, using the girls as a pretext.

The only thing that is a bit worrisome for her is that she has begun seeing Andoni as an outsider. Just today, he walked into her workroom to bring her a coffee and he stood there, as if he had forgotten where he was. The person numbly looking at her, thinking of who knows what, seemed a complete stranger to Iris.

Andoni was furious when Iris began applying the new rules. Saturday afternoon and once again Andoni is nowhere to be seen. Iris goes to the park with the children. Andoni calls her.

"You guys are not home."

"No."

"So where are you?"

"Try to guess."

"Are you going to start playing games now? Guessing games?"

"I play them all the time when I try to guess if you'll show up or not. I don't like it either."

Andoni lost it, he accused her on the phone of blackmailing him, he claimed that he had the right to know where his daughters were and kept going on and on.

Iris would like to erase Andoni like she does on the phone, by pressing a button. The thing is that the daughters ask about him. Andoni is wonderful with his daughters. They go to have ice cream, he pushes them on the swings until they get exhausted, and they enjoy their unhurried time together. Andoni does not have any other responsibilities and lives with no set schedule. The girls tell Iris, "Don't get mad at Dad." Iris has promised herself that she will eliminate anger from her life. She does not want to live in anger nor let anger accumulate inside. It is Andoni's call: he either accepts her rules or that's it. With the boundaries she has established outside, she has earned inner space for herself. She has regained her strength and she gets to determine the road to follow without letting someone like Andoni have a say.

While she is waiting for Alex, Iris feels in control of herself thinking that she has pushed Andoni as far as possible from her life. While her daughters have been young she has had little urge for sex, and on sporadic occasions when she did, she satisfied it by herself. As things have returned to normal, her physical cravings have also awakened.

The rolling of the thunder has stopped and Iris feels an impulse to open the window. The quivering branches of the willow in the courtyard seem to want to spank the rain. But the rain is the indisputable power and dominates all. As if thrust by the confusion of the storm, *something* hits Iris. At full speed. Iris is not sure if it is pushed by the storm or if it flew inside. It seems to teeter. Zigzagging like a drunk, it hits the window frame and comes into the room. It is black, dark. It is stumbling madly among the colorful leather pieces hanging in Iris' workroom. "It's alive," is all Iris can think, "it's alive." It looks like it is about to fall to the floor but unexpectedly it jumps and is able to escape out the window. Confused, Iris looks out the window but can't see anything. She wonders for a second if it was a bat, but she discards the idea at once because bats do not usually fly in the rain. She shrugs her shoulders and shuts the window tight.

She returns to grab her glass of wine and hears Alex parking his car at the courtyard. "I must tell Alex what just happened," she thinks, amused. The sound of the doorbell startles her. "It can't be." She is puzzled. Alex has his own set of keys. He only comes at night when the girls are in bed. Iris walks to the door, weary. She wonders if it will be Andoni coming in anger and desperation to break the peace. She opens the door firmly and sees two people in front of her. "They look like two towers," she thinks. Her senses are working slowly and she looks attentively at the two strangers. A man and a woman dressed in uniform. As Iris begins realizing what this might be about, the woman begins talking.

"Are you a relative of Andoni Ekiza?"

Iris tightens her mouth, as if doing so would help her answer a question like that. The woman in uniform does not have patience and begins to talk once more.

"Excuse us, but we would like to talk to a relative or to someone close to Andoni Ekiza."

Iris relaxes her right knee and shifts her body weight onto her left thigh. Iris figures the woman's second utterance is better formulated, but "close" is not the correct term either. They hear the car tires rolling into the courtyard. "That's him," thinks Iris. "That's Alex's car." The three of them look in the direction of the headlights and when they turn off, Iris recognizes Alex's form, downcast due to the rain. Iris's left knee is about to give out and she rests her eyes on Alex when the woman declares, "There has been a car accident."

UXUE ALBERDI ESTIBARITZ

Elgoibar, 1984

A writer and an improvisational poet, Uxue Alberdi Estibaritz has also worked as a radio announcer, interviewer, and a translator. In 2006, she won the Xenpelar improvisational poetry award and in 2008, the Osinalde improvisational poetry award for youth. She narrated the Basque version of Paul Gallico's *Snow Goose.*

She has published three literary books: *Aulki bat elurretan* (A chair on the snow, 2007), a collection of short stories and *Aulki-jokoa* (Musical chairs, 2009) which has been translated into Spanish as *El juego de las sillas* (2011) and *Euli-Giro* (Sense of Chagrin, 2013). She has also published children's literature, including: *Ezin dut, eta zer?* (I can't do it, so? 2010), *Marizikina naiz, eta zer?* (I'm messy, so? 2011), and *Txikitzen zaretenean* (When you get smaller, 2012) The story "Gifts" was published by Susa in the fall of 2013. She is the youngest author in this anthology.

Gifts

We pick up the roasted chickens and are off. I told Truko three times that today is not the best day to go but he insists we must.

"Mother is waiting," he explains.

The thermometer reads ninety-seven degrees. The ultrasound photos stick to the envelope, about to melt. Who knows, what I'm carrying in my womb might melt too. The white might mix with the black and it may dissolve into a gray smudge.

It's been ten minutes since we left Bilbao and the warm aroma of chicken has overtaken the car. I lift my hand to cover my nose but still, I retch. I tilt my head back and try to fall asleep, hoping we'll arrive soon. We are on the road driving seventy miles per hour and headed to Altzate, Truko's family's farmhouse where he was born. He drives slower since I am pregnant, in silence. All he says is, "Mother is waiting."

We are going to Altzate to celebrate that the ghost in the ultrasound photos has a penis. That is why we have the six roasted chickens in the trunk. The fetus weighs nine ounces but I have already gained thirteen pounds.

When we went to have the twentieth-week ultrasound, the nurse said: "If it doesn't have a penis, it's a girl."

I was lying on the exam table; I lifted my head toward my inflated stomach and asked:

"Instead of identifying half of the world's population by exclusion, can the ultrasound reveal a vagina?"

"Excuse me?"

"Nothing."

Later, when she spotted it, she said: "Aha! There it is."

I sensed relief in her voice, a hint of pride of someone who has discovered something important. America, penicillin, an appendage inside my womb.

"Shit," I said.

"What?" said Truko surprised.

"I lost the bet."

The aunts in Altzate could not be more certain.

"It's a boy," the three of them declared in unison.

They sat on the wooden bench placed against the old farmhouse, looking up. Every Wednesday, my youngest aunt's daughter-in-law plucks their eyebrows and while they looked upward in the direction of the strings of peppers hanging from the house's façade, drying above their foreheads and while I was still walking toward them, they assured me: "It's a boy. "

The daughter-in-law smiled and I contradicted them to show them that they could not know more than I in matters of my own womb.

"They always guess right," the daughter-in-law warned me.

After we drive past the Durango tollbooth, I ask Truko, "Will six chickens be enough?"

He wipes the sweat off his forehead and shrugs his shoulders. The chicken smell is suffocating. I open the window but the chicken aroma mixes with the stench emitted by the paper mill. The stifling heat inside the car blends with the sultry air outside. I quickly press the switch to close the window and we remain inside the car, trapped in the heat and our pungent body odor.

I wonder what the penis means to Truko's family. The only thing I can think of is going once a year to the wineries in Rioja and the men remaining quiet while the women talk. That is the only thing that comes to my mind. And then, it just occurs to me: I might not like my own son. The thought crosses my mind for the first time.

As soon as we park by the house, we see it, "Welcome Beñat," a banner with blue letters hanging across the farmhouse façade.

"Who's Beñat? A liberated prisoner coming back to town?" I ask Truko.

Truko looks the other way and begins getting out of the car. If I remember correctly, we mentioned once that if we ever had a boy, we might name him Beñat. Maybe. But as soon as they see us get out of the car, Truko's mother and her sisters begin jumping up and down, cheering, "Hurray for Beñat!" Truko's father and two uncles regard us from the bench in the back. The wives wave colored balloons. I notice that they have hung a Basque flag by the door. It reads, "Hurray for Beñat!" on the white cross of the flag. The heat is insufferable.

Truko walks in front of me resembling a shadow attracted by the farmhouse's invisible pull, a faithful horse unable to escape the force of gravity that the birth home exerts on him. Today's celebration at Altzate is more about having us there than celebrating that our baby has a penis. *Welcome Home* in big letters—that is what this is about. If it were possible to reproduce children the way plants do, they would sow seeds in the field in front of the farmhouse, so little Barrenetxe babies would grow, right there, where grandmother's ashes were scattered.

"Hello," I say, "We brought the chicken."

Truko kisses his mother and his aunts. They continue jumping and shouting, more discreetly now. Their voices entangle and I can only decipher a few of the words they say. Stout. Grandmother. Gifts. The uncles tap their *txapelas* and lift their chins, as if asking, "How's it going?" Truko pats each of them individually on the back. "All is well," I decode, *whack-whack*. No words. He looks at his father; they stare at one another for a moment and each pulls a cigarette out of his pocket, which they will smoke on the bench by the main door. I am not sure if father and son have a synchronized choreography or if they are two astronauts in a far off planet smoking inside their space suits, their senses immersed in smoke. They look convinced that, amid all the things around them, smoke is the most interesting on which to focus. After they finish smoking their cigarettes, they remain sitting a yard apart, their gaze fixed on some far off point on the horizon. No one knows when they decided to stop talking to each other, what day, or why, but it is clear that this is a pact made among men, a trench amid women's conversations, a respectful sign toward the women. The patience displayed by the men in this family is truly shocking. They are so still that you would think they would do something unexpected.

"Very good, Añes."

Mother takes the bag with the chicken from my hand. She adds:

"It won't be enough, but don't worry, I have a big pot of stew ready."

We brought six chickens. There's nine of us. The thermometer reads almost 104°F.

"Come with us," the four sisters tell me, "we have something for you."

They bring me into the house. The kitchen is full of presents and there is something in the air, a feeling of an eternal Christmas that makes anyone feel like a child. The four of them are observing me.

"Open them," they order me.

I know what I am in for. I shiver. They keep scrutinizing me.

"See if you like them. We bought them thinking of you."

I should not open them but I do not dare antagonize the four sisters. Where is Truko when I need him?

I knew it. I told him so. This is how it starts, with gifts. I think of Truko's brothers' girlfriends. All the couples live in the new houses they built next to the farmhouse. They are all neighbors, dwellers in the modern houses they erected on Grandmother's land. Brothers, daughters-in-law, and grandchildren, all confined in 2.47 acres. All the Barrenetxe family members piled up together with their wives. All of them. They accepted the gifts: The house slippers, to feel comfortable in Altzate; Silk pajamas for when they stayed overnight. Tooth brushes, tampons, and hair straighteners. All the sons' girlfriends had to do was ask for something, and it would be gift-wrapped at the next visit. They accepted the gifts and in return, they received the gift of intimacy, which came tethered with an umbilical cord that allowed them to move, at most, one hundred yards from the home of Grandmother's birth.

"I'll open them later, I promise. I need to go to the bathroom now."

I am not sure why I said, "I promise." So dumb of me. I

look for Truko while I am headed to the bathroom, but all I hear in the house is the rattling of the sisters. The men must still be outside. It is unbelievable how quiet the men in this family are. Almost mute. I lock myself in the bathroom and call Truko on my cell phone. I am going to tell him that I am sweltering amid the sisters and ask him to open the gifts. But he does not answer. He must have left his phone in the car.

As I sit on the toilet, I open the window that looks at the old, stone sink in back, and light a cigarette. A few kiwi trees, a hawthorn, and some fig trees surround the old outdoor stone sink. I see the doghouse to which Adi, the dog, is chained all day long, and see a swing hanging from the sturdiest branch of a fig tree. I picture a blond boy yanking a stick from Adi and swinging from the fig tree; stretching his body in an effort to reach the farthest fig hanging from the branch with his fingertips; picking kiwis with Grandfather and making tasty kiwi preserves with Grandmother; catching red colored fish with his hands in the old water trough and looking for bird nests in trees. He looks happy. I flick the cigarette butt into the toilet; I pull the flush chain and go to the dining room. I feel more relaxed now. Truko might be right, I might be making too much of the situation and, after all, the four sisters might not have any ulterior motives.

"They just want to show us how much they love us, that's all," he told me the last time we visited Altzate.

On that previous visit, after lunch, as we were having coffee, they broke the news that they would give us one of the apartments as a gift. On a mundane Tuesday. Truko did not budge. That is what happens when you are used to receiving gifts. After Grandmother's land got expropriated, the agreement stated that each grandchild would be awarded one of the apartments built on the property. And apparently they had fixed up one for us with some money they had secretly set aside for that purpose. They dangled the keys in the air.

"Thank you," said Truko "but for now we are happy living in Bilbao."

He said, "for now," even though we had decided long ago to live in Bilbao; even though we were about to take out a loan; even though we had decided our son was going to grow up in Bilbao. At that moment, I despised my boyfriend. Weak, I thought, soft, such a coward.

"It's up to you," said the sisters in unison.

And as we were walking up to our car, they asked:

"When will you be back?"

"Soon."

"Did we say something wrong?"

I knew without a hint of doubt that the questions were meant for me. But I did not answer. I let Truko use his diplomatic skills.

And once again, we are back.

By the time I walk into the dining room, they are all sitting at the table. Each one in their assigned place: men facing women. Truko sits facing his unmarried aunt and my seat is next to hers, on the edge of the table, which creates an ugly asymmetry. The seating arrangement makes it look like my partner is about to arrive, is going to kiss me and is going to sit at the empty space next to Truko. Grandmother's empty chair presides over the table. Truko's mother stands and looks first at Grandmother's empty chair and then at my stomach, she says:

"If Grandmother were alive."

I can't decide if she says it as a statement, a wish, or a threat. I am not sure if the expression should be followed by three dots, an exclamation mark, or a period.

"Sit here," she says.

She offers me her chair, the one with padding on the seat and the back. I appreciate her gesture, she wins me over because I know that seating arrangements are not taken lightly in Altzate but I prefer to take my usual spot, the guest's seat.

"Thank you," I say and as I say it, one of my neck muscles relaxes.

"Have you been smoking?"

"No."

She catches me off guard and brings her nose near my mouth. Everyone is staring.

"Yes, I smoked a cigarette in the bathroom," I confess.

I am not sure why but I direct these words at the men; probably because I know they will not respond.

"You ran out of toilet paper," I inform them.

Truko's mother is still standing in the middle of the dining room and begins making senseless gestures as if she were restraining herself from slapping something, a word, the air, perhaps. She opens her mouth but no sound comes out. Truko gets up and, holding his mother gently by her shoulders, makes her sit down in her chair. As soon as she takes a seat, she begins serving the salad mechanically while Truko uses the opportunity to inform everyone how good my pregnancy is going. He says that the initial fear I felt is gone now. He tells them what I shared with him in bed the night before I had my first ultrasound: that I wondered in fear if my womb were empty. That I was afraid the nurse would look at the ultrasound and say, "there is nothing here." He chuckles a little, "*that's Añes*," he says and plants a kiss on my cheek. Then, he adds that I get up four times at night to pee.

"She'll be the best mother in the world."

One of the aunts gets up from the table.

Then Truko's mother says:

"'Mother,' that's sure an easy word to say. A mother must sacrifice everything for their children, isn't that true Añes? Once a mother, always a mother."

"Once a mother always a mother?" I ask myself. These sentences that seem to hold a hidden meaning frighten me. What is the meaning of "mother," "*ama*"? What is this word that reads the same forward and backward? I wonder what *everything* means for Truko's mother. And for his mother's mother? And for my deceased mother? Truko's grandmother sacrificed her health. "She has worn out her bones. This woman has worked too much," said her doctor. Truko's mother sacrifices sleeping in order to cook a week's worth of meals for her son. My mother, on the other hand, died without ever having filled a Tupperware. And her naptime was sacred. She was a painter and she paid another woman to do the housework and to take care of us: to protect her intimacy. I was twenty when she died.

"If I'm leaving," she murmured in my ear at the hospital, "it's because I already taught you everything I was supposed to."

Everything. All. I knew, though, that I had many things left to learn from her. But she must have wanted to die believing she had given me *everything*.

"Want soup?"

If nothing else, my mother was practical. She did not wait for anyone to die. Nor did she wait to live. If we die as we live, it occurs to me that Truko's mother will die serving soup.

The aunt that left the dining room earlier returns.

"I remembered that I left the window open in Grandmother's room and I went to shut it," she says as she goes back to sit down in her chair.

Grandmother's bedroom is on the first floor. It has been seven years since she passed away but she still has *her room* in the house; they have not touched anything since she died. Her clothes hang in her closet, her shoes stay put away in boxes, and her walking stick rests on her bed. I know that Truko has visited the room before and opened the closet to smell Grandmother's scent. She still has *her room* in the house and, not only that, but she is the one still making the most important decisions in the house. Even today. Whenever they are faced with having to make a big decision in Altzate, one of the sisters invariably asks, "What would Grandmother say?" Once, when they were in the process of selling some land, I heard them debate; when the youngest sister's son had a woman from Nicaragua as his partner; when Truko's oldest brother decided to change the Christmas dinner menu. "Don't you even think about it," she would answer from her death-room. And no one in Altzate dared to bring up those topics ever again.

There is a story that Truko has told me many times, the one about Grandmother's ashes.

When their mother died, the sisters could not seem to agree about what to do with her ashes. Keep them? Scatter them? Where to keep them? Where to scatter them? Finally, they ended up dividing them. Half of the ashes were buried in the cemetery next to Grandfather's remains. Each sister set apart a bit to keep in lockets hanging around their necks. And they scattered the rest around the roots and surroundings of the oak tree, which stands in front of the old Altzate farmhouse. But fall is unpredictable and this time it acted out by sending a blast of wind right at the moment when they were scattering the ashes. They ended up flying toward Truko and covering his pants. Truko instinctively shook them off. Later at night, he put them in the washing machine and wore them three days later.

I thought it was odd when he first told me the story, how a body can be divided after death, that is. One-half buried in the cemetery, a bit dangling from her daughters' necks, a part under the home oak tree, some more in the grandson's pants, some in the washing machine . . .

"Now, whenever I wish to talk to Grandmother," Truko confined in me, "I'm not sure where to go. She's everywhere. And nowhere at the same time."

They bring the chicken to the table, and another aunt gets up. We hear steps on the upper floor and ten minutes later she returns with the gifts.

"We'll open them with dessert," she says and places them next to me.

"We were talking about Grandmother," they explain to the aunt that just came in.

She smiles, and the sisters look at each other.

The men ingest the last pieces of chicken.

At once it occurs me. I see it on their faces. She is alive. The idea darts through my mind. Grandmother is in her bed, alive. How could I have been so gullible? I observe the sisters, then Truko. I am a hundred percent convinced of it. She's alive. Otherwise, why all these comings and goings? The leftovers they say are for Adi and the daily habit of cleaning Grandmother's room? Footstep noises, open windows, and the constant need to mention Grandmother?

I remember the time when I got up from a nap to go to the bathroom. Although Grandmother's door was always closed, on that occasion I found it slightly ajar. Truko's mother had left the bottle of bleach and the window cleaner by the door, in the hallway while she cleaned the bedroom. Under the buzzing of the vacuum cleaner, I heard her talking but, silly me, I thought she was talking to herself while remembering her mother. Now I understand all the movements during mealtimes, the aunts getting up and leaving, one after the other, and the silence of the men, weak accomplices. Truko, how did he dare?

"Bring the cake," says one of the sisters.

"The gifts," the other two chime in.

Adi, the chained dog. The daughters-in-law that pluck the aunts' eyebrows. The dangling keys. The Basque flag. The ashes. *Open them.*

They place the gifts on my lap. Truko passes them to me one by one. Inside the colorful wrappings I find little pajamas, towels, little beanies, crib-sheets, and bibs, all with the letter *B*, the name *Beñat*, or the initials *BB* embroidered on them.

One of the aunts gets up. Footstep noises.

It is time for coffee.

The men smoke cigarettes and cigars.

I don't dare light a cigarette.

We raise a toast to Beñat.

Soon after we bid them farewell.

Truko puts the gifts in the car and kisses them all, one by one. I sit in the car and fasten my seatbelt. I see the Basque flag through the rearview mirror and the banner still hanging, and the four sisters under it waving goodbye. Behind them, in silence, the three men.

A gust of wind. We're off. Bilbao should be getting closer.

KARMELE JAIO EIGUREN

Gasteiz, 1970

*K*armele Jaio Eiguren is a journalist and writer. She published her first work, a collection of short stories, *Hamabost zauri* (Fifteen wounds) in 2004. In 2006, she published a novel, *Amaren eskuak* (Mother's hands) that received many awards; including the Igartza Award, the Zilarrezko Esukadi Award, Zazpi Kale, and Beterriko Liburua, the award that the reading public confers to the best book written in Basque. Amaren eskuak has been translated into Spanish as *Las manos de mi madre*, and into German as *Mutters hande*. It was also taken to the big screen in 2013 under the direction of Mireia Gabilondo. In 2007 Jaio Eiguren published the story collection, *Zu bezain ahul* (As weak as you) and in 2009 the novel *Musika airean* (Music in the air) which was published in 2013 in Spanish as *Música en el aire*. In 2010 she published a selection of stories from *Zu bezain ahul eta Hamabost Zauri* into Spanish under the title *Heridas Crónicas* (Chronic wounds) and in 2012 she published the collection of stories titled *Ez naiz ni* (It's not me). She adapted the story "Ecografías" ("Ultrasounds") into a play which was directed by Ramón Barea and premiered in 2010, interpreted by Irene Bau.

Ultrasounds

*I*t happened on March 8, 2007. I remember the white light on my face. I remember mouth-less faces, hands between my inner thighs, latex fingers penetrating my body. Voices. Relax. Push now. Not now. Breathe. Pressure on my temples, on my abdomen, on my inner thighs. When the contraction comes, push; push as hard as you can! I remember the smell of disinfectant and the scent of blood when I split in two. All done. All done. A few seconds of darkness. The light on my face once again. The faces are back, the fingers, though now removed, feel as if they are still inside me, stirring my entrails. And the voices. Congratulations. It's a beautiful baby girl.

I remember everything perfectly. Everything except the crying. I remember almost everything except the baby's cry. No matter how hard I try, I can't remember it. I can't imagine it, because in reality, none of this ever happened. It never happened. I was never admitted to the hospital to deliver a baby, yet I remember it as if it had happened because I have dreamt of it so often; I pushed so many times in my dreams . . . without ever having been in a delivery room. It is possible that having my sister Elena work at the Cruces Hospital as a midwife and having listened to her stories might have helped me imagine the moment in vivid detail. Perhaps having been born in a farmhouse and having witnessed calves and sheep being born since I was a little girl might have helped too. But truth be told, I have never experienced a contraction in my life even though my body has contracted time after time in my dreams.

᭱ ❦ ᭢

The trip was long. I left from the Loiu airport with my sister Elena on February 23. We flew to Frankfurt where we took a connecting flight to Addis Ababa. But the real journey began about two years ago, if not earlier. It might have begun the first day I dreamt that they took me by ambulance from my apartment in the old part of the city to the Cruces Hospital and there, in the delivery room, I gave birth to a baby. It was the same day that I dreamt something inside me was pulsing, a heart, and it was not mine. The day I began hearing the echo of my womb and feeling cold outside of my dreams. The most real things that happened to me during the last two years have happened in the world of illusions. Reality has been nothing but the framework to construct the dreams that I have inhabited.

The journey has been long and hard. Two years of rough seas. And amid the train of waves only one thing has remained steady and still before my eyes: a photograph. These last months I have clung to this photograph as a castaway clings to driftwood. Amid the surge, with all my strength, I held the photograph of a girl gazing back directly into my eyes. She has been my lifesaver. My shelter during storms of reality.

As soon as we took off from Loiu, I thought I physically felt the contractions that, until then, I had only experienced in my dreams. It was a Friday morning and I remember looking through the window at the green, damp mountains surrounding Bilbao, at the cars that, like colored ants, advanced toward the coast, at the foam of the Cantabrian sea tracing the coastline, and at the red roofs scattered on the mountains.

"Do you see it? Can you see it?"

My sister kept jabbing her elbow into my shoulder. I tried but I could not make out the roof of our farmhouse in Aulestia—the farmhouse where we grew up and our parents still live. It was impossible to see it. The large house hid among the mountains that emerged from the earth like women's breasts. And in my hand, all this time, the photograph. The dark eyes of the girl growing bigger along with her quizzical face.

"And who are you?"

My sister did not want to leave me alone at a moment this delicate. "You have enough to worry about getting into this all by yourself," she told me when I shared with her that I had started the adoption process. At least I would not be alone on the trip. Elena, always my older sister. Like when she would accompany me on Saturday mornings from the farmhouse to the parish church in Aulestia, where they prepared us for First Communion. She would wait outside until the class was over so she could walk back home with me. That morning in the airport, I felt the same, as if Elena were accompanying me to catechism class once again. There are women that are mothers before they ever give birth. My sister was already a mother many years before she had Mikele and Jon, when she accompanied me all the way to town along a road that got covered in mud when it rained. I still remember the brown puddles. I remember her open hand to which I clung with the strength and inertia of a magnet.

"You have enough to worry about getting into this all by yourself," she told me. She reminded me of Mother when she objected to my decision. As if it were a whim, as if it were unnatural, as if I defied the world with my obstinacy in giving love and shelter to another human being. As if not having a man by me would prevent me from becoming a mother. The same as when you go to the window of some bureaucratic office and a gray voice tells you: you're missing a stamp; you're missing a picture . . . You are missing a man, everyone implied it with their eyes. And they made me feel as if I were missing an arm. As if I were not whole. As if I were half a person.

"At least you won't be alone on the trip," Elena told me showing pity on her face. As if implying: You don't know what you're bringing on yourself. I never looked at her with pity during either of her pregnancies. On the contrary, every time she held my hand to place it on her stomach and asked me, "Can you feel how it moves?" my heart would speed up and I would smile at her, full of excitement.

"This is the leg. Do you feel it?"

As children, we pretended to be mothers so many times in the farmhouse as we stuffed our sweaters with dried leaves. At that time, we did not know that there were different ways of becoming a mother. Whenever she showed me Mikele and Jon's ultrasounds, she would ask me, "Who will she look like?" It never crossed my mind to look at her with pity. Nevertheless, she did, the very first moment I told her I had begun completing the paperwork to adopt. No one in the farmhouse looks with pity at the cow that nurses a calf whose mother has died during labor. It's something natural. I tried to explain it to them so many times.

It caught me by surprise to see Ethiopia from the sky. For the last two years I had envisioned a very different landscape from that of my childhood. Somehow, it looked greener than I expected. More like our land than I had imagined. The color and the freshness of the eucalyptus trees welcomed us. And the light. The light was definitely different.

The reaction Elena had when I told her I had started the adoption process was nothing compared to the reaction my parents had. Mother tried to ignore my decision until the very end.

"You still have time to try to find a partner, so you have a baby as God intended it."

"Don't do this to us," she told me with her eyes. Father did not even mention the issue. He disappeared every time the topic came up. He ran away making excuses. He had to feed the cattle, clean the barn, or gather the hay. He did not understand anything. "From Ethiopia?" Mother would ask. I am not sure if she asked me, or someone above her.

"African?" she asked, turning her eyes up toward the ceiling of the house, where strings of dried peppers hung.

Yes, a black child. The black sheep of the Aulestia farmhouse.

"It takes a long time to process the forms, Mother, and it could be a while before . . ."

My mother hoped that during the waiting period I would reconsider, or I would meet someone, or I would get back with Gari. He was always an option. Mother never understood why we broke up. She says that today men and women look each other over too carefully and that if you look at someone long enough, you will always find some flaw, that no one is perfect, and that a bird in hand is better than . . . That is what Mother says. She says that in her time they did not dwell on it so much and that married couples stayed together like God intended. Like them. I have often asked myself if Mother and Father were ever in love or if they just felt affection for each other as result of coexistence.

The sun in Africa is different. The light is different. I realized that as soon as I got off the plane. The light in people's gaze is different too. White and clean. A woman holding a sign with my full name written on it waited for us at the airport of Addis Ababa. When I saw my name written so far away from home, I felt it did not belong to me, as if it were someone else's name. That did not seem the same name the teacher in the school in Aulestia called every morning while taking attendance or when she asked me to recite the seven times-table, that stupid seven times-table. I felt that at that very moment I began entering another woman's body. Like a snake, I was beginning to shed my old skin that now felt like a mere shell to enter a new world, a completely unknown world.

A man waited for us outside the airport in a 4x4 truck, his strong black arm resting on the open window. The woman who greeted us accompanied us to the hotel and to the orphanage the next day, in the same truck with the same driver. On our way, her forehead was sweating. I remember her frown, her cramped teeth. Her name was Mamo. She did not tell us much more than that she was going to accompany us during our stay in Ethiopia. When she opened her folder, it surprised me to see a photograph of the Brandenburg Gate, in Berlin glued to the inside cover.

"Have you ever been in Berlin?" I asked her, pointing at the picture and smiling at her, relieved to have found a topic of conversation to lighten the mood and break the tension created inside the car.

"No, never," she answered abruptly, closing her folder at once.

When my coworkers found out about my adoption plans, everyone was curious. It was so exotic. Something new they could tell their spouses when they came home.

"And what is she like? How old is she? Do you have her picture?"

"She is between one and two years old, though the exact birth date never got registered."

"What's her name?"

"Amina."

"Is she pretty?"

"In the photo she's beautiful."

She was beautiful in the photograph. I wore it out looking at it so much, night after night, while lying on my bed in my new apartment in the old part of Bilbao. I was holding the photograph in my sweaty hands when we drove to the orphanage. I kept passing it from one hand to the other so I could dry the free hand against my pants. I was sweating like Mamo. I was sweating like I did before I met with the social worker who would decide if I would be a fit mother. The first interrogation after which someone would determine if I deserved to be a mother.

"You don't have a partner?"

"No."

"Have you ever had a partner?"

"Yes."

Those appointments to consider my eligibility tilled my inside, as the plow tills the soil. While each question, sharp as a knife, undressed me from within, I pictured my father cultivating the fields. I thought of my father with his eyes fixed on the soil, tilling it furiously as if wanting to bury the words that remained bottled up during an entire lifetime. All those untold words that are starting to hurt him.

"And are you planning to have a partner in the future?" she asked me, holding the report while looking at me from above her glasses.

Had I known the answer, I would have said something. But I did not say a word. I threw my hands up and thought: "That's it. I'm not eligible."

During the suitability sessions I met some couples that were going through the same process.

"And they didn't make both of you come?"

"No, well, I'm by myself."

"Ah."

I knew that look. It said something like: "You don't know what you're getting into."

❧ ❦ ☙

Mamo walked us inside the orphanage. On our way in, she talked to us like an automaton about documents, stamps, and hearings.

Bureaucracy. Not a single word about our trip, about how we felt, about the child. Not a smile, not a gesture of complicity. Mamo, who never let go of the folder, talked to us without looking us in the eyes.

When we entered the orphanage, I felt as if the white stares of the boys and girls peeking out from the rooms pierced my clothes. The same way wild wheat-heads stuck to my clothing when I played with Elena as a child. We used to run in a field, spearing each other with wheat-heads that stuck to our wool sweaters. Elena and I laughed, laughed at the world and the sun. Years later, Elena and I find ourselves entering an Ethiopian orphanage. All in the same lifetime.

I remember children's babbling, distant crying, and the smell of porridge. And the serious, dry expression of a nurse that crossed our path. And the dry, serious expression of the government representative that waited for us. It was the same expression Mamo wore. Finally, after entering a room, I saw the little girl, sitting on a blanket spread on an examination table, her dark eyes interrogating me. The same eyes from the photograph.

"And who are you?"

They say that after giving birth, women forget the nine months of pregnancy, that they leave them behind like a faraway memory. I don't remember what happened during those two weeks I spent with my sister in Addis Ababa very well either. I just remember spending hours with the child before returning her to the orphanage, singing to her, because our nervousness did not allow us to do anything else. Somehow, we needed to discharge the electricity that was constantly generating within our bodies.

"*Kalean gooora, kalean beeehera . . .*"

She looked at us as if we were extra-terrestrial. We must've looked ridiculous to her moving our arms up and down, following the rhythm of the song. She stared at us but did not make any faces, did not smile, did not cry. Serious, like the nurse, like the government representative, like an adult. Like Mamo. And every time she stabbed me with her cold gaze, I felt an empty echo, the sound of fright—like metal against metal. A cold, dry clanking.

"And who are you?"

She asked me with every look. "May I know who you are and what you are doing here?" I cried my eyes out every night while I was there. I cried from the tension I felt because the papers did not arrive, the last stamps were not getting stamped and because from the fear I felt anticipating the moment we would bring the child home with us. It scared me to death to think of that moment. And if she doesn't want to come with me? And if she rejects me? I remember those days and my fear in a blur, as if they were hidden behind a window covered in raindrops.

ᶳ ❦ ᶳ

Gari always wanted to have children but, at that time, it was I who thought the moment was not right. Getting pregnant would have meant a drastic step backward in my career. I would not have made it to the position I hold now had I decided to have a child then. I have regretted it occasionally. If I had had a child with Gari, we could have been happy, perhaps. Having a child could have filled the gap that arose in our relationship. But with time the gap began to get bigger and deeper until it turned into an insurmountable chasm. We were two islands in the middle of the ocean. He found it hard to understand that I wanted to be alone. He was convinced that there was a third person, someone I had substituted for him. But after twelve years together, ten years living under the same roof, it did not take another man for me to realize that Gari was an empty well.

"You don't love me anymore?"

"That's not it."

"Then . . . what's his name?"

"There's no one."

Truly, there was no one else. Just a dry well I feared to peek into in case I fell in. It felt the same as getting too close to a cliff. The fear of falling makes you stumble into the void.

I saw him again after I began the adoption process. I invited him for coffee to my new apartment so I could tell him about it. I preferred to tell him myself instead of having him hear it from someone else. I felt obliged.

"The apartment is small but it looks good. The living room furniture piece fits perfectly there. It looks different now . . ." Gari kept looking around the apartment as if searching for a trace of himself. He was checking to see if there was something left of him in my life, a photograph, some reminder of the twelve years we spent together.

I told him; he listened, and, for an instant, I thought I saw water at the bottom of the well. I thought for a moment that he understood me and that he even felt overjoyed by my decision. We were sitting on the sofa. He brought his open palm to my cheek and, almost without thinking about it, I kissed him. I kissed him like in the old days when we lived together, and instinctively, we ended up embracing on the sofa. At that moment I realized that it had been two years since anyone had hugged me, and when I felt his warmth, my eyes filled with tears. Then Gari kissed my chin, and smiling, with the expression of someone who has a great idea that will solve everything, said:

"You don't need to do this alone. Don't worry. I will help you. We'll do it together."

And once again I saw the dry well. I realized that he did not understand anything. I had held onto the wrong life preserver. Gari could not save me from the heavy seas. I had to swim on my own.

"I'm sorry, Gari. I want to do it alone. Do you understand?"

We told each other goodbye with a cold kiss that smelled like tobacco. Gari smoked only when he got nervous, when he did not know what else to do. I felt guilty when he last looked at me. I had become a selfish person who did not want to share anything. I had even ended up with his records, with the piece of furniture that had stood in our living room for ten years, and now I was not even going to share the love of a child.

In Ethiopia there is a doctor for every 36,000 inhabitants. That is what the driver of the 4x4 told us one day when Mamo had us wait for her with the car running, while she took care of some paperwork at the consulate. He told us that, during the last year, more than three thousand doctors had left the country. Among them, Mamo's husband. Lowering his voice and making a face as if he were telling us a secret, he told us that Mamo's husband was now in South Africa where he went looking for better pay. That he abandoned her. That other colleagues had left for Botswana and the United States. He kept shaking his head as if to say: these are difficult times.

Mamo came out with the papers in her black folder. Each look she directed at me blamed me for the situation her country was going through. Each look accused me of coming to rob them of their most precious possession. Robbing them of their future, their boys and girls. Everyone was running away and those that did not got taken away. But I decided that she did not have the right to look at me like that. It was her line of work. She was involved in it too. She earned a living helping others take away their children.

"Do you have children, Mamo?"

She directed a piercing look at me, swallowed and continued talking about papers and stamps, consulates and governments, the child's passport, and what we had to do when going through customs. Her forehead still sweating. I offered her a handkerchief. She rejected it.

I remember the conversations I had with Elena at the hotel, lying on the bed, gazing at the ceiling like when we were children and went to bed in that room with walls made of stone. We would run from the warm kitchen, go through the freezing hallway and once in the bedroom, we quickly got under the blankets. Since those days when we used to share our secrets, we hadn't spoken again like this, like two sisters.

"Do you think Mother will understand it?"

"Do you know what she said when she learned you were going to go ahead with this? Why did you need to come this far to get a child? That it was like breaking the natural order of this world . . . That what these people needed was help and not people taking their children away."

"I don't think she worries about me bringing a child from another country but, rather, doing it on my own. If I were with Gari, I don't believe she would object.

"Speaking of which . . . How's Gari?"

My sister also would have preferred that I had tried it with Gari. She did not understand why I was doing this on my own either. Or at least she did not understand it until she embarked on this trip to Ethiopia with me.

"Do you know what?" she said, "Looking at you from here . . . I swear you resemble a woman about to deliver a baby. And I know what I'm talking about. I have seen many . . ."

I was not sure if she was teasing me.

"Do you want me to teach you how to breathe? It works very well during labor."

I remember all the laughing at the hotel, bordering on hysterical laughter, discharging our tension. I remember breathing deeply and blowing out all the air in laughter. I remember Elena's look, which I hadn't seen since we used to laugh about everything, from giving nicknames to boys, to the way we looked when we played dress up with Mothers clothes, to using the lipstick that aunt Bego from Ispaster brought in her purse because Mother never used make up, not even on Sundays to go to church. Elena. I had almost forgotten who my sister was. I had almost forgotten who I was, who I had been. The scent of both of our beings drifted through the bedroom of a faraway hotel in Addis Ababa. I had forgotten such a scent.

"Doesn't she ever smile?" I asked the nurse while she dressed Amina.

She did not answer. I am not sure if the lack of an answer was because she did not understand me, did not want to understand, or because the answer was obvious.

She did not smile. She never smiled. Her face was a constant question mark. And each time she looked at me, it felt like a slap in my face. With each look I would begin regretting everything. I felt guilty for taking a child away from her surroundings, like someone getting a souvenir from a place she visits; for not wanting to share her with anyone; for not having tried to have a baby like God intended, as Mother would say; for having rejected Gari . . . for everything. I even felt guilty about hunger in the world.

Every day we took her out of the orphanage, she looked back, at the serious nurse, at that damp building, at other boys' and girls' white gazes that we left behind. I was afraid she would begin to cry, that she did not want to come with me. I felt as if I were forcing her to become my daughter when we did not really have anything in common, not even the color of our skin. Perhaps Mother was right, I might be doing something unnatural, something against the natural order of the world, something nature would end up making me pay for.

"Why do you think she doesn't smile, Mamo? Is it us?"

Mamo did not answer. She looked at me as if wondering: why should Amina smile? Wondering if I would smile if I were in her situation. That night at the hotel, I dreamt that I was a child, sitting on a haystack in our barn. Neither Father nor Mother were there, only a black woman with Mamo's face who was going to take me to her country. I kept looking at the farmhouse and then, in fear, at the black woman who smiled at me showing her white teeth. She stretched her black arms in my direction and sang to me. I only felt like crying and when she took me in her arms, I looked back for Mother, Father, and my sister that I couldn't see. I did not smile either. I was overtaken by fear just like Amina. I wanted to stay at the barn, trusting that Mother would appear at any time. Yes, Mother would come. Mothers always end up coming.

Elena called home every night. She asked Josu, her husband, about Jon and Mikele.

"Put them on the phone."

She talked to them every night. Every night they asked her when she would be home. She had never been apart from her children this long. I felt guilty about that too. As we were lying on the hotel bed, tired but unable to sleep, I asked her:

"Is it true that when you see the baby after labor, you forget the pain?"

"That is a lie . . . The same lie as when they say that you feel like the happiest woman alive after labor."

"It isn't true?"

"We are told many lies, you know? No one tells you that you'll cry your eyes out when you arrive home with the baby, and that you'll feel less energy than a withered plant. Or that you can have feelings of rejection toward that being that cries nonstop and that prevents you from being the person you were before . . ." Elena had her eyes fixed on the ceiling, stretching her arms and scratching her elbow with her hand. "No one tells you that after the brutal exit of the baby, you feel like a plastic hand emptied you from within and, while at it, took a part of your soul. There is a big lie that we women nourish and perpetuate as if not wanting to discourage others. And the secret ends up hurting us. I see the eyes of women leaving the delivery room. They think that the suffering has finally ended. They do not know that the biggest aches are still to come."

"But not everything can be untrue . . . There must be something very special."

"No, everything is not a lie. There is one big truth. That even though they physically cut the umbilical cord, it remains; it never disappears completely. You always hold a rope that leads you to your children."

A rope. Like the one lassoed to a mule. I thought of Mother pulling the mule with her body leaning forward. She pulled away from us like that too until we grew up and now we are the ones who have started pulling away from her. She's getting old. You always think your mother cannot grow old, that she'll always be there, always ready to take care of you. But one day you look at her and you notice that she has dwindled, that her eyes look smaller and that she does not ask you about everything you do like when you were a child. However, you are aware that every movement you make provokes a reaction in her muscles, like when the doctor taps your knee to check your reflexes. A rope. You always hold the rope that leads you to your children. That is what my sister told me.

"You turn into a sort of bell," Elena said. "It feels as if

your children are tied to the rope hanging from the bell. Each of their smallest movements makes you ring; it makes you react, without intending to. Your children hang from your forever. And I think that sometimes they move just to make sure the bell keeps ringing. That it's still there."

I remembered the sound of the bells of the church in Aulestia. My parents in their Sunday best, walking toward the village, guided by the sound. Each bell toll moving the world.

Elena prepared a bag with the clothes that I would take to the orphanage the next day. I remember having seen Mikele dressed in them. Elena knew what Amina should wear. What would fit her well. At that point in time, Elena was the only mother in the room. She became a mother at a very young age, when she accompanied me to catechism class on Saturday mornings, long before she even had her own children. I still feel the magnetic pull that connects my hand to hers.

I did not sleep at all the day before we got Amina. The day before I became a mother. That night I wondered at what exact moment I would become her mother. Was I already her mother because the documents had been signed, or would it happen after we left Ethiopia? Mamo accompanied me to the orphanage. Elena stayed at the hotel packing. Mamo observed me while I was dressing Amina in the clothes I had brought from Bilbao. Her old pajamas would stay in the orphanage; they would be passed on to another child. Seeing the empty pajamas on the bed was like watching the ghost of a child. As if performing a magic trick, I was going to make a child vanish from there. Mamo kept looking at me with a combination of sadness and hate. I could not get the child's arm into the sleeve. And Mamo kept watching me, without showing any compassion, without offering me her help. Perhaps the child's arm was not made in the size of my world's clothing. Perhaps the child was not made to fit my world. Mother could have been right when she said I was about to do something unnatural. I was afraid of hurting her arm and could not get it inside the sleeve, and she began to cry. And Mamo kept observing, without moving a single muscle. The child's cry was getting louder and I felt as if a steel beam were going through my throat. And I exploded. Now the child was not the only one who was crying. Then Mamo, after pausing for a few seconds, walked up to me and helped me get her arm inside the sleeve. The little girl quieted down immediately.

"Thank you, Mamo," I said, wiping my tears with my forearm.

She did not answer. She handed me a handkerchief. I took it. I remember her forehead sweating and her hands once again grabbing the black folder that she had left on the table to help me. She held her folder against her chest, as if she were holding a baby.

She came with us to the airport in the same vehicle she had picked us up in. Before boarding the plane, Mamo came up to me. I was holding Amina in my arms. She did not even acknowledge the child. She had her eyes on me. A piercing gaze. It was the first time she looked me in the eye. I had not felt Mamo this close during my stay in Ethiopia. She was silent for a few seconds then, finally, said:

"I had a daughter too. I was sixteen . . . You asked me."

Her words took me by surprise since she acted so distant and cold during our stay. I thought that, like my father, after swallowing all those words and feelings, she had felt the coldness of the steel in her stomach. And instead of burying words in the soil, like my father does with his plow so no one sees them, Mamo had decided to release them.

"At that point in time I couldn't take care of her and they took her, like this, like her," she pointed with her finger to Amina but she did not look at her, she did not want to look at her.

"I'm sorry . . ." I apologized, feeling guilty, as if the child I was holding were hers.

"They took her to Germany, to Berlin. I began working with adoptions so I could find out where they took her. And I did finally find out, but I still keep working here."

"I'm sorry."

"I lost a daughter but found a job," she said, with an ironic smile. The first smile since we arrived in Ethiopia.

I was at a loss for words. Suddenly I recognized in Mamo's eyes the blank passages framed by the Brandenburg Gate. And I thought I heard a faraway bell. A mournful toll.

"Goodbye, Mamo."

She did not answer. I gazed at her while she walked toward the vehicle. Empty as a balloon.

It was very hot inside the plane. Amina's forehead was sweating. Then I remembered that I had Mamo's handkerchief inside my pocket. The plane took off and, while looking through the window with Amina on my lap I imagined that land of mountains and eucalyptus trees crammed-full of mothers wringing their empty breasts. Mothers aching and crying while in labor. Bells tolling incessantly. Bells sobbing. Screaming in despair. Sweating foreheads. With no handkerchief.

"Are you OK?" asked Elena.

"Yes." I did not dare tell her I was feeling a fitful, deep ache in my abdomen, as if they were contractions.

Both of us looked at Amina who remained serious and

expressionless, until Elena got up to go to the restroom.

"I'll be back."

At that exact moment, Amina looked at me and something happened that will make this moment endure forever in my memory. It was March 8, 2007. Amina lifted her right hand and brought it up first to my chin and then to my lips. I could not stop trembling. Then she lifted her other hand and with one hand on each side of my mouth, stretched my skin, as if looking for a smile on my stone face. Then, she embraced my chest with her arms and began looking for a comfortable position on my bosom, until she fell sleep. Right then, I felt my breast dampen, leaving a trace in my bra.

I never had a contraction in real life and yet, I delivered a child. It happened on March 8, 2007, at thirty thousand feet above the earth. Torn up from within, as only a woman in labor could be, with my daughter nestled next to my stomach; my daughter tried to remember the time she spent inside my body, curled up in my dreams, before they took us both to the delivery room.

I remember the white light on my face, the voices. Congratulations. It's a beautiful baby girl.

IRATI JIMENEZ URIARTE

Bermeo, 1977

One of the first stories I ever wrote was titled "Maite eta txoria." "Maite had a bird with feathers, beautiful. It sang well. But the lion came and ate the bird. Maite cried a lot. She loved the bird."

I wrote the story when I was six years old and if someone were to ask me now what I have learned about literature since, I would say "not much." Someone has something and loses it or looks for something and cannot find it. If you succeed in connecting the reader with that someone, you're set. You must find the words that you need and erase the ones that are obstacles. Ah! And write as if you were six years old: without forgetting it's a game. That is the method I followed to write a few short stories and longer works of fiction. The short novel titled *Bat, bi Manchester* (One, two, Manchester, 2006) tells the story of two young men who meet away from home, and become close. *Nora ez dakizun hori* (You who have lost your way, 2009) and *Atsekabe zaitut* (I pity you, 2010) take place in contemporary Bilbao, but the main characters are vampires who work at a radio station.

I also have published nonfiction, a Malcom X biography for young readers (2002) and a gender-perspective review of the television series *The X-files* for example (2011).

I have always enjoyed television, films. . . . That is the reason I studied audio-visual communication and have worked steadily in radio, television, and on the Internet.

                   ❧ ❦ ❧

I still try to write with the same joy as when I was six. Maybe with a little bit more craft. At least, enough to explain where the hell the lion came from.

Tears of the Orange Peel

She was fourteen when she last saw her grandmother walk. Her teeth, her skin, her final exams in June, and the shy responses given to her mom, were all fourteen years old. Each of her guffaws were fourteen years old, her wild angry moods and foolish rages (that came from nowhere and went nowhere.) Fourteen years looking in the mirror. Fourteen years old were her feet, fourteen her breasts. But not everything in her was fourteen years old; her hands had fallen behind.

"Look at your hands," said Grandmother from the bed. "You're fourteen years old and look," she sighed sickly, motionless. "You still have the hands of a child." Later, Grandmother spoke not for her granddaughter but for herself, with her eyes half-closed as if dreaming, "For me, you're a child." She felt her hands and her heart pulsing. Now she was fourteen and young, (nothing but opportunities before her), now she was a three-year-old child (everything seemed frightening, overwhelming), once again fourteen, now forty, now fourteen times fourteen, one hundred and ninety six (she pictured herself old, as if she knew it all). Fourteen, infinite, dancing away, swinging on the thread of time in unison with her heartbeat. Systole-diastole.

I wish to grow; I don't wish to grow.
I wish to grow; I don't wish to grow.

Grandmother's heart was not healthy.

"It is covered by a layer of fat," said the doctor.

She had fat all over too. She had been fat ever since childhood. Well, somewhat overweight. Chubby. That's what the woman who went to buy bread at her mother's bakery always said. "What a beautiful, chubby child." And then, instead of buying bread, they would buy pastries or sweet-smelling buns, croissants for breakfast, warm, fresh baked. Except during school hours, she spent her time there, next to the oven, like a cat longing for warmth. Always there, next to her mother while her father was gone, at work, away from home. "Father?" she often asked. "At work, sweetheart." Always the same answer. Father was always at work.

As a child she spent countless hours with her *amuma*; right there, by Grandmother's skirt, under her wing, under her protection. "Easygoing, eh?" said the ladies at the bakery. "She is such an easygoing child." They said it as a compliment but she did not understand what they meant. Easygoing? She was not easygoing at all. She was not fond of the outside world, the real world, the one outside her shell. It was such a frightful place, that outside world, so desolate. Fortunately, she did not need it; her head was full of voices that kept her company.

She had a friend who lived right there, in her mind. They read the same books and sang all the TV tunes together. (The videotape was ruined, it was old, it always got caught at the same point; they couldn't care less, they knew them all by heart.) Sometimes Mother would send her to run an errand and she always felt shy and entered the neighborhood store timidly. Her friend would hold her hand with her invisible fingers and tell her "don't look at people; lower your little head; buy what Mother told you and pay for it; just like that, well done, we'll watch TV when we get home; you don't need to look at anybody."

"Each heartbeat requires more effort than it should," explained the doctor after he completed the check-up.

Grandmother was weak and frail (that is how she would remain, though the doctor did not say it, they heard the untold words loud and clear). Her heart was trapped in fat, systole-diastole. Too big of an effort. At fourteen, fifteen, sixteen she felt like that too, beating inside her soft shell. She did not want to venture out. But sometimes, sometimes, not always, she felt like getting out.

> *Sometimes I want it. Sometimes I don't.*
> *Sometimes I do. Sometimes I don't.*

They told her at fifteen what she had known for a long time. As when she was a child, she still loved drawing. Her chubby hands and full fingers were always filthy with ink tears shed by her pens. She was scribbling on the pages of a used notebook when Mother came up to her. Her hands resting on each other looked like a multi-colored riddle, a kaleidoscope. Mother told her that Father would no longer be living at home. Not to worry and not to cry. That he would love her the same.

"I know," she said staring at her hands in order to avoid looking at Mother's eyes.

The world was a strange, distant place. She was often surrounded by people yet always felt alone. Life was nothing but noise coming to her from far away. Right there, in front of her mother, she could hear the cars outside her window, people's comings and goings and her parents' words from a long time ago echoed in her memory ("you're never home" / "when I get home you sure don't welcome me") everything was noise to her. Her mother hugged her and asked her if she was alright. She replied yes, she was fine. If she had told the truth, she would have said no. She felt as if she were hovering over her own body, watching herself, as if in a photograph.

"I'm the child of divorced parents," she thought. A sentence. That was all. She lived far from that sentence, inside her shell, in an underlayer, safe. Hidden, in a place where nothing hurt her. She wanted to break her shell and get angry at her parents. Yet, she wanted to remain in her shell, calm, far from heartache.

> *I want to scream. I am well.*
> *I am well. I want to scream.*

At sixteen, she lost twenty kilos.

She dropped the first four as result of salmonella, then the next three when she quit going to the bakery and the ones between seven and twenty, from her own willpower. All of a sudden it was twenty and even though in her mind she did not think so, she looked slim. She felt like the fat girl that took the place of a slim girl and she wanted to know where her twenty kilos had gone. By then her grandmother looked like wrinkled cigarette paper. Her eyes flickered languidly and showed their white orbits as if she had rolled them inward, toward her head instead of outward. Once in a while, still, she would get up in the middle of the night and come to Grandmother's bedside and listen to her breathing. "Grandmother, don't die," she kept thinking.

"Please."

But she knew Grandmother would die, and in order to get ready for that moment, each time she began to tell her goodbye, she felt guilty and returned to bed, shivering (at twenty kilos lighter, she was often cold). Suddenly, Grandmother rolled her eyes from inside her head out and said, "You look different." When she explained that she had lost twenty kilos, "Oh my, twenty kilos," Grandmother mumbled. "My child, do you realize how heavy a twenty kilo sack of potatoes is, twenty kilos of rocks, twenty kilos of meat?"

"Where might they be?"

She did not know. The physics classes she hated so much taught her that nothing dies, *all matter transforms*. Therefore, she should ask herself not *where*, but *what* the twenty kilos were now. She did not share her fear with anyone but she was afraid. Afraid of having burnt with her kilos a part of her that she should not have lost. When she began losing weight she could feel her muscles, shivering. Systole, diastole, beating. And once, suddenly, her heart felt angry. She was at the bus stop when a salt-and-pepper-haired guy looked at her. At her. Straight. She looked away, too soon. Her ears turned red, cheeks flushing.

> *Don't look at me. Please, do look.*
> *Please, do look. Please. Don't.*

At fourteen, thirteen, fifteen she did not like to look at herself in the mirror. After she lost the weight, when she looked, she did not recognize herself. When she was out on the street, she couldn't find her image reflected in the storefronts. In her dreams she saw dead cows in the Mundaka estuary. She got in her car but the road was made out of butter and she could not get it going. The sky was an orange peel and when she asked the friend who inhabited her mind for the meaning of her dream, she did not get an answer. She felt alone, lost. She looked like a thin parenthesis but deep inside she was still a fat child; the fat child whose hands were stained with ink; the beautiful child who lowered her gaze, the one who read books at recess time. She missed the twenty kilos. Her shell.

"Gosh, you've lost so much weight," her father said when he saw her after many months. He held her by the waist and hugged her tightly. She felt as if she had been hugged for the first time in her life, she felt small in Father's arms. She felt weightless. She could fly. She felt that if she were to fall in the water, she would not sink, as if she were strong enough to lift her father in the air. For the first time, she thought of those twenty kilos as heavy. Worthless.

She contemplated herself in the mirror, for the first time. And there she saw it. Her face. Her childishness lost, her cheekbones more noticeable than ever, protruding as if someone had sharpened them with a razor. It took her by surprise to find her mother's image hidden in her face. It was true. The ladies that used to come by the bakery, when they met her on the street would now tell her that she resembled her mother. Look at who surfaced under the twenty kilos. Mother.

"Now we look like Mother," she told the image reflected in the mirror.

The mirror agreed with her. And that night, when she came up to Grandmother's bedside, she saw Mother's features in Grandmother too. She realized there was a chain, linking all women. She was Mother, and Grandmother, and Grandmother's mother, and Mother's granddaughter. And it did not matter how much weight she had lost, how much she changed. She was always going to be part of that chain, just another link, but she still had her place in the world, she was someone.

Precisely, when she noticed the guy at the bus stop looking at her, she thought, "I'm going to look at you" and she felt her own rebirth with her daring look, her heart racing, frightened, happy.

> *I'm changing. I don't want to change.*
> *But I'm changing. I am.*

The day she turned seventeen she realized that the child was dying.

Everyone told her, "You look so much better now," and although everyone said it with good intentions and felt happy for her, she did not hear that, instead she heard "you were fat before. You were fat before and I didn't like it. I didn't love you." No one said, "Where are the twenty kilos? Why did you lose them? I liked them." Only Grandmother, no one else. And then she realized that Grandmother was the only one who truly loved the child and she felt a traitor's guilt, a bitter taste in her throat. *I changed intentionally. I am the one who killed the child.* She was a good child, a beautiful, fat child; she had a pure gaze, full fingers, warm hands. She never hurt anyone; she was Grandmother's beloved child but Grandmother would die soon and then no one would miss the child.

> *Not even myself. Yes, I will.*
> *I will too. I won't either.*

Grandmother died at eighty-two.

At midnight, she heard footsteps. Since Grandmother was bedridden, it prompted her to get up, barefoot and in her pajamas. She called, "Amuma," but did not get an answer. When she entered the kitchen, she found her right there, sitting down at the table, wearing her robe, emanating the same smell she remembered from her earliest childhood. "I have scrubbed this very kitchen four hundred and ten thousand times," Grandmother told her, "can you picture how much dirt that is?"

"Where do you think, my child, that all that dirt has gone?"

She did not have an answer for Grandmother and gently hugged her and murmured, "Amuma." She did not feel like saying much, the word "Amuma" summarized it all, "I don't know where all that dirt and things we don't need go. I don't know." She heard a whisper in her ear, "child, my beautiful child." They remained embraced for a long time in silence until they got lost in the embrace and consequently her heart awakened and repeated, "I love you, I love you." By the morning, Grandmother's heart had stopped and the doctor informed them, "She didn't suffer." Grandmother's legs were stiff. When she asked the doctor if she could move her, he replied with an emphatic no.

"I would guess she died in the evening. Right here, immobile as she has been these last years."

Of course. She had been dying over a number of years. Sighing, gasping, better today, worse tomorrow, old age. Today she was dead, tomorrow not so dead. Slowly. Dying kept the same rhythm as life. Systole and diastole.

> *I love you Amuma. Where have you gone?*
> *Love, where have you gone Amuma, I love you.*

Grandmother died but she herself had been the one that killed the child. She was older than seventeen but still saw her reflection as a fat child. It was about time.

"I can't stand it anymore," she told her, "go away."

From the other side of the mirror the child asked her:

"Where will I go? Where do children go when they are raised and forgotten by people?"

She did not know and did not answer back. "Go away!" she repeated and then cried for half an hour. It might not have been a half hour because when crying, real time does not exist. While she was mourning her lost childhood, she felt as if Grandmother and she were in the same place, keeping each other company, the child and Amuma. While thinking those thoughts she lost the other twenty kilos. Those twenty kilos everyone has, even slim people, sometimes to their deaths. When she began living without her nostalgia she understood that the child was really dead. She understood that she also would die and though at first the thought made her feel nauseous, she understood. It was necessary. The child that she had been once had to die. And when she died, something else would blossom instead. "We are nothing but a heartbeat, systole and diastole in the Universe," she thought.

Where do the dead go? Where are the twenty kilos? What happened with the dirt in the kitchen? It was no longer important.

"Go away."

I'm here. I live.
I'm alive. I'm here. Beating.

KATIXA AGIRRE MIGUÉLEZ

Gasteiz, 1981

*K*atixa Agirre Miguélez is a writer and professor of media studies at the University of the Basque Country.

She published her first book in 2007, *Sua falta zaigu* (We need a light) a collection of short stories. In 2008, she was awarded the Igartza Scholarship to complete her second collection of short stories; the book was published in 2009 under the title *Habitat*. She has also written three children's books *Paularen seigarren atzamarra* (Paula's sixth finger), *Ez naiz sirena bat, eta zer?* (I'm not a mermaid, so?) and *Patzikuren problemak* (Patziku's problems). In 2010, she created the series for young adults *Amaia Lapitz*, which narrates the stories of the adventurous archaeologist Amaia Lapitz.

Some of her stories have been translated into Dutch and Catalan. In the spring of 2015 she will be publishing her first novel. The story we have selected is one of six stories that comprise the *Habitat* short story collection.

Guy Fawskes's Treason

Now we live in a one-room apartment, more precisely, in a one-bathroom apartment. Which means that in the morning we must share. Joseba gets up first and takes a shower. When he is done, he ties the towel around his waist and yells: "done!" Then, I reluctantly get up, downcast, and step into the shower while he gets ready to shave. He says that with the steam from my shower, his pores open up and it is easier for him to shave. He swears by it.

We both finish about the same time, I with my shower and Joseba with his shaving. We both are particular about matters of hygiene. Occasionally, Joseba complains that I shower with too much hot water, fogging up the mirror. "Didn't you ask for steam? So there you have it!" He mumbles. I hardly pay any attention to him. He tries to wipe off the mirror with a towel. He complains again, but I don't listen to him. And, all of a sudden, ready. We are clean and almost awake: it's no small feat. We both get dressed then have breakfast and, finally, head to our stupid jobs. (I am actually the one going to work because Joseba was fired two months ago. An investment firm bought out what, for the last four years, had been his company, and surprise! He is currently unemployed, poor man.)

Now we live in a one-room apartment, more precisely, in a one-bathroom apartment. We haven't always. Joseba used to live with his wife amid several rooms and two bathrooms. I lived alone, with no need of two bathrooms. At that time we did not share a bathroom. Usually, when we were together, I used the shower alone, while he stayed in bed. But often I had to leave without taking a shower because his wife would call to let him know that her flight had been moved up and that she would be home earlier than expected. Then, rushing, I would take off and leave Joseba behind, changing sheets, opening the windows, telling me goodbye with a fake smile, bye, bye, yes, will you leave, already?

That was Joseba's wife's obsession. Calling. From airports, work, or taxis. Giving us heads ups. I never understood why she did it. She made it so easy for us, really.

Well, that is until that one time when she did not. She made it home a day early, by surprise, with no warning phone call. "Darling, I'm home . . ." neither of us heard the key turning. I was in the bathroom, had just gotten out of the shower and was drying my hair. Joseba was lying in bed, half sleep. At least she did not catch me in bed. But if I think about it, it has to be just as daunting for a woman to find another woman in her bathroom, blow-drying her mane of dyed hair.

And this is how we have ended up here, in this one-bedroom, one-bathroom apartment. In what had been my single woman's place, now condemned to share it with a man.

I bought this place when I was twenty-seven, much earlier than most of my friends, soon after I signed my permanent employment contract, taking advantage of the low interest rates. It is located ten minutes from downtown and it has a kitchen, living room, a bathroom, elevator, and central heat. I was supposed to live alone in this place. That was the plan after my then-boyfriend took a long time to consider his options and finally decided that he preferred to continue living at his mother's. I am, or rather, I was as proud of this place as if I had built it with my own hands. Then Joseba showed up in my life, and, then, Joseba lost his place. And this is how we find ourselves every day sharing a bathroom.

Although the statement above could convey a hint of resignation, I do not complain. I am not like those who have it all and are never satisfied. I wanted Joseba and I got him. Good. But there are, certainly, a few things about this new situation that I do not appreciate. The shower situation, for example. Picture the scene: Joseba wearing a towel at his waist, holding his razor in his hand, and me, naked, unprotected, defenseless. Joseba knows it and takes full advantage.

"Next week Vic will be gone for work." If he mentions a place, I cannot hear it. "She'll be gone from Monday to Thursday. I told her we'd take Terry."

I did not fully understand what he said because when he has his face covered in shaving cream, he hardly opens his mouth to talk. And besides that, I had just turned up the water pressure so I could rinse the last of the soap off my body.

Nevertheless, I answer, "OK," and my mouth fills with water.

"But, don't you remember that next Monday I'll be gone too, to Madrid for that job interview?" No, I did not remember that. Vic out of town, Joseba out of town, and Terry in our place. With me. I frown, but he does not see me behind the shower door.

Vic is Joseba's ex-wife. When Joseba and I used to have sex in their bed, on the sheets ironed by his wife and in view of their Christmas family portrait, her wife's name was Victoria. Pronounced with every single letter. Victoria just called.

Victoria is driving me crazy. Victoria, Victoria! When we were discovered, when his wife threw him out of their house, when she restricted how often he could see their son, when she turned most of their friends against Joseba, as if by magic Victoria became Vic. And in the most hurtful situations Victoria even turns into Vicky. I can't understand why this friendly tone now.

I do not like it.

Terry is Victoria and Joseba's son. The reason he has such a ridiculous name is that Victoria is originally from England and because the child (in her opinion) deserved an English name. The poor boy's full name is Terence Mikel. They did not realize that his middle name (Joseba's modest triumph), instead of improving it, made the whole situation worse. He is eight years old and I can't stand him because he is more intelligent than I. He knows it, too, and makes it clear time after time.

Do not misunderstand me: I am not stupid. I have always been a good student. I completed a master's and I am a logistics manager. You can tell by my title alone that I hold an important position with my company. Logistics manager. I am respected at work; the logistics operators fear me, and my assistant admires me. In five minutes I can organize a fleet of trucks and prepare two transatlantic ships for departure. Truly.

But, without a hint of doubt, Terry is more intelligent than I. I've known him since he was two and a half (that's when I got involved with his father) and even then I was able to tell that this precocious child was somehow different. He was only two when Joseba and I took him for a stroll (at that time Joseba and I were at the initial phase of our relationship, it was nothing but a chaste, amiable friendship). He didn't approve of me and frowned at me; he knew I was not trustworthy, an intruder, the witch prostitute who was about to destroy his perfect family's harmony. The boy knew it; I know he knew it. We understood each other and yet, we could not stand each other (these are not incompatible feelings). We still feel the same today.

Nevertheless, I told Joseba OK, without realizing what I was getting into, although I should have known that my eyes stinging from soap did not foretell anything good.

I wish I could say that when I got involved with Joseba, I did not know he was a married man or that he had a child. That I was tricked, enticed, that I was young and inexperienced. That is not true. I knew it. I was aware of it. My head hummed. Incessantly.

We met at the gym. He was the only male in my aerobics class. And not only that but surprisingly, he was very good at it. He followed all the steps correctly; he kept the rhythm and did not sweat much. I assumed he had no interest in women, that is until I saw his wife and son waiting for him after class, which made me feel overjoyed. After our aerobics class we coincided in a spinning class and later in a body-pump class. (Of course, it was not pure coincidence. By then I had gained the confidence of the secretary at the gym, which made it easy to follow Joseba's whereabouts.) Sometimes, after class, we would wait for his family at the gym's bar, drinking sports drinks.

Once he brought his son to the gym. He explained the circumstances: his wife was gone for work, yes, she was often gone on business trips (even though he directed the information to the whole class, I took it as a personal message directed to me). Usually, a babysitter took care of the child but she was sick today and he had to watch after him, and

since he did not want to miss the last body-pump class . . .
He left poor Terry in a corner of the room, strapped in his
stroller, holding onto his pacifier. The child did not open his
mouth, did not cry, and did not complain, not a peep during
the whole hour. Probably because of the bewildering scene
he was witnessing.

After class, the three of us took that stroll I mentioned
earlier. A short one. I realized during that stroll that Terry
was able to foretell everything. And I was proven right when,
a few months later, everything unfolded as he had envisioned.

I would love to say that I felt bad for Joseba's family, that
I felt guilty, that I scourged myself every Sunday afternoon
to reduce my guilty feelings. But it is not so. After all, from
the time I was a child, they taught us that all is fair in love
and war. Besides, let's be clear: if anyone messed things up,
if anyone acted deceptively and callously, it was Joseba. By
law and in the eyes of the world, he was the committed party.
He was the one who signed documents swearing loyalty and
fidelity to his wife. (I won't be too harsh on him because he
has paid dearly for his offenses: court appearances, having to
move out, restricted child visitation, and now, when things
were on their way to getting settled, he loses his job.) But
when it comes to me, why should I have a guilty conscience?
I was single, free like the wind. I was free to do as I pleased.
And that is what I did.

☙ ❦ ❧

Terry is not a normal child. For one thing, he has that ridiculous name. For another, his intelligence and suspicious wit
feel threatening to adults. And finally, he does not attend a
regular school. He attends the British School complete with
manicured gardens and full of children dressed in uniform.

Terry is one of those children wearing a school uniform. He must wear a tie every morning. Once again, this is another of Victoria's triumphs. There is no equal to her country's education anywhere in the world. She is so convinced of it that she will not send her son to one of the ikastolas, public schools, or to one of those old religious schools.

Most of the children attending the British School are of British descent or have snobs as parents, and then there are the poor children who suffer both burdens. In that school they do not mention Olentzero or Tartalo. Children don't sing "Pintxo Pintxo." Instead, they draw King Arthur, and they are told who knows how many senseless facts about the British monarchy. Once I saw one of Terry's drawings: there was the Queen wearing her crown and even holding her scepter while inaugurating a new parliamentary session. I thought it was strange but I did not mention anything to Joseba.

That darned school is far away too, in the foothills, located at a prudent distance from the lumpenproletariat neighborhoods. For the last two weeks the buses have been on strike, so I have had to drive all the way up there to get Terry. I was already nervous about picking him, the driving only got things worse.

I stayed a bit away from the fence together with the South American nannies, unlike the real moms who go all the way through the manicured gardens. Occasionally, I have come with Joseba, and even in those cases I stay on the other side of the fence. Joseba tells me not to be stupid and to go with him, but I never do, never, just in case.

This is the first time that I'll come alone to wait for Terry. He knows that I am the one coming today. I'm sure that he has a surprise in store for me.

All the children leave the school building running and causing a ruckus; they snatch the sandwiches their nannies have brought for them; they remind each other, screaming, of the awesome cartoons on TV at six. All the children, that is, except Terry. He leaves school calmly, his backpack on his back and a drawing in his hand. He kicks a pebble and dismisses a friend with a lift of his chin. He sees me but he does not change his pace nor does he acknowledge me.

"Hi," he tells me when he sees that he has no other choice and walks up to me.

"Hello, Terry" I reply in Basque. "How was school?"

"Not bad," he answers in English.

"Are you going to talk to me in English?"

I speak English. I use it at work almost daily because our company's headquarters are located in Southampton. I completed an International MBA in Madrid, which was entirely in English. My friends are convinced that I have great fluency and are jealous of me because they still have to enroll every September in very expensive language academies. But I cannot speak in English with Terry. Ever since I met him, I have always spoken to Terry in Basque and that is how it's going to be. This decision does not imply any type of militancy about the Basque language. If I were to talk to Terry in English, he would laugh at me. In silence, yes, his indifference would be swept away by an ocean's undercurrent, but he would laugh at me. Paranoid? No. I have already mentioned how we get one another and how subtly we hate each other too. Although it may seem that I am going too far by saying this, I must admit that if I had been born under his circumstances, I would act the same way. I know I would laugh at a busybody witch who spoke my mother tongue haltingly. I might've been like him, yes. Smart and cunning. Sharp and introverted with adults (some adults, anyway). Suspicious.

Realizing that my last question is a rhetorical one, he begins scanning around for the car.

We haven't started off on the right foot, no we haven't.

We get in the car, begin driving off and Terry does not
utter a single word, in English or in any other language. I
divert my eyes from the road for a minute, and look at him
through the rear mirror. He is not a very handsome boy. His
ears are wide, he has his mother's sickly, pale skin, sprinkled with freckles extending all the way from his chin to his
neck. (I want to think that Terry's ugly features come from
his mother's side and not from his father's. This way, I reassure myself that when I have a baby with Joseba, he will be a
beautiful child.) Nevertheless, his gaze is not his mother's or
his father's. It is his own gaze. Sharp and almost sad.

"We can go anywhere you want to have an afternoon
snack, and later, if you don't have any homework, we can go
to see a movie . . . What do you think?"

"I don't have any homework; I already finished everything in school. But they're not showing anything I want to
watch."

"What about a snack?"

"I always have fruit for an afternoon snack. You have
fruit at home, don't you?"

And with that, we head home, with no more words uttered. At least he is no longer talking to me in English. It is
only ten after five. I predict a long and difficult evening. I
have heard that children go to bed early. Nevertheless, in our
home, the sleeping part is a problem. Terry's bedroom is our
living room; we open the sofa and he sleeps there. (When I
bought the sleeper sofa, I did not anticipate our guest would
be Terry. I pictured visitors from abroad, and exciting, erotic

encounters.) Victoria thinks the sleeping arrangement in our apartment is horrible and has come up with the most ridiculous excuses for Terry not to stay overnight with us. Nevertheless, she is calming down a bit and now he regularly stays two weekends a month with us. Since Victoria travels a lot (though not as much as when Joseba and I met) we get extra visitations often during the week too. He is familiar with our place. I believe that he could not care less. Once, at the very beginning, he asked his father how come the house was so small. Joseba was caught off guard and did not know what to answer. It happens frequently. He often does not know how to answer his son's questions. It has happened to me once too. "Where is the yard?" he asked me suddenly, holding his soccer ball under his arm.

But by now, he has accepted the small size of our apartment, having to sleep on the sofa, not being able to play soccer, and he doesn't waste time worrying about his surroundings. He moves quickly through the hallway, making sure we do not notice him, most likely because he does not want to be here and because it annoys him to leave any trace of his presence for future archeologists. We have reserved a shelf for him in the living room bookcase. For his things. His things consist of four or five volumes of Shakespeare's works. I took a look at them: *Hamlet, Othello, Julius Caesar,* and *King Lear.* He has the children's illustrated editions, from the series *Shakespeare Can Be Fun.* Although Terry has begun to ask for the original versions for adult readers.

We keep his few items of clothing in a drawer: a couple t-shirts, his uniform shirt, the school tracksuit, and some underwear.

He loosens his tie, as grown-ups do, and sits on the sofa. I am convinced that he mentally does everything he can so his body does not leave any indentation on the sofa. His legs dangle. Boredom takes over his face. I sit on the armchair next to the sofa, close, too close.

"May I have a banana?"

I go to the kitchen to get him what he wants. I also hand him a mandarin orange and a yogurt.

"Thank you," he says.

If nothing else, he's been well taught. We must thank the British school system for that.

In an effort to break the silence, I ask him one of those questions that neither of us are interested in but one asks a child in an effort to treat him as an adult.

"What did you do in school today?"

I anticipated one of the following: nothing, got bored, what's it to you? Or even the three of them at once. But no.

"We talked about November fifth."

I was floored, I did not expect a five-word sentence and I felt a spark of hope inside.

"November fifth?"

"Today is November fifth."

"You're right."

Is that what they do at that British school? Teach them what date it is and talk about it?

"Remember, remember, the fifth of November . . ." sings Terry in English lifting his dangling legs to the side, his mouth full with a bite of banana. "You don't know that song?"

Do I look as if I attended a British school? I don't tell him that but I shake my head to clarify what he already knows, that I don't have the slightest idea about that song or any tradition behind it.

". . . the gunpowder treason and plot, I see no reason why gunpowder treason, should be forgot . . ." he's not looking at me, his gaze is lost somewhere else, still chewing on his banana.

"That's a good song," I told him with no conviction. "What is it about?"

He gets up off the sofa and goes to the kitchen to throw the banana peel in the garbage. If the floor were full of sand, he would not leave tracks in it, he moves so lightly, like a classically trained dancer. When he gets back, standing up and with his hands on his hips, he says:

"Then, you don't know anything about Guy Fawkes?"

I run a quick search through my mind. I'm looking for Guy Fawkes. Who is he? Please, Guy, if you are somewhere in there, make yourself known. Will he, perhaps, be a character in one of Shakespeare's plays? I must confess that I have never read any of Shakespeare's works but I know the most famous ones, like everyone else. I know who Juliette, Mercutio, Othello, Lady Macbeth (Macbeth's wife that is) are. But who is Guy Fawkes?

At the end, I am going to have to admit it.

"I don't think so. Who is he?"

Terry sighs and returns to the sofa. His body seems heavier now because the sofa sinks somewhat under his bottom. Is he finally lowering his defenses? He is holding the mandarin orange, very focused on the sticky peel, and I think that he forgets about Guy and me. But no.

"Guy Fawkes tried to blow up the Parliament in London when the king was present in the year one thousand six hundred and . . . five. Exactly, the fifth of November in one thousand six hundred and five. He was Catholic, Guy I mean, not the others. The king, for example, was not Catholic. He was James the First and he was pro . . . protestant. He belonged to another religion. That was why he wanted to kill the non-Catholic people, including the king. And that is why he engineered the plot."

Sometimes Terry astounds me when he lashes out with one of those, "exactly, on the fifth of November in the year one thousand six hundred and five." But other times, for example, when he talks about Catholics and Protestants, you can tell he does not know what he is talking about. And that relaxes me immensely. It reminds me that I am dealing with a child and that I am a grown woman. What has always amazed me is the fact that his parents treat him as if he were an adult. Especially his mother. But Joseba does it too, perhaps by pure imitation.

"My dear, I had such a bad night, this headache has kept me awake," Victoria might say to the child. "Terry, do you think it is worth going to the beach today? It looks like it is going to rain," Joseba tells him, after the child has already put his bathing suit on and grabbed his towel and beach toys.

But that is not the most amazing thing. What it is really shocking is that Terry answers like an adult. "Mommy, I told you a thousand times that you should take your pill as soon as you feel your headache and not wait until it is too late." "You are right, dad; they announced on television that it will keep raining until tomorrow." And he leaves the room to take his swimsuit off, without throwing a fit.

But I refuse to do the same. I fight the idea that I am in front of a small-sized adult.

"So what? Did Guy achieve his goal?"

"No way," he looks offended. "Don't you know that the Parliament has endured to this day?"

"Yes, you're right."

"The Parliament is located in London."

"Yes, it is in London. I've visited it."

"Guy didn't achieve his goal. They caught him in the Parliament basement with a bunch of barrels full of gunpowder. How do you say gunpowder in Basque?"

"Bolbora." I'm relieved I remembered it.

"Yes. They caught him when he was about to light the barrels but he wasn't able to do it. They caught him and accused him of high treason. At that time treason was the gravest offense. There was nothing worse than that. That is why his treason is known as the 'Gunpowder Treason Plot' and it's celebrated every year on November fifth, today."

"And what happened to Guy?"

"Do you want to see my drawing?" he asks, ignoring my questions. Nevertheless, I must admit that his offer pleases me.

Of course, I tell him yes, that I can hardly wait one more second to see his drawing. He finishes his mandarin orange, wipes his hands with the cloth I give him and runs off to get the drawing he left on the chest of drawers at the entrance. When he returns, he shoves it in front of my face and holds it there.

"Here, Guy, the traitor, and those are the barrels, full of gunpowder."

He is right. There is Guy, wearing black trousers and a stripped jacket as well as a tie and a hat. In that British school, apparently, they have not taught them yet about seventeenth-century dress code. In the drawing, Guy is about to light one of the gunpowder barrels with a match. In order to make clear that the barrels are full with gunpowder, Terry has drawn a label that reads, "Gundpowder". He has drawn poor Guy with a mean face, a cruel smile and his eyebrows diagonally directed toward his nose. The picture foretells Guy's fate, as hinted by the open door on the right and a foot stepping into the room that he has drawn. The foot of authority. It looks like the explosion will be prevented.

"It looks good, Terry! We can hang it on the fridge, or we can put it right there on the television set if you want."

"Thank you, but I prefer to take it home."

Touchée.

The first time Joseba brought him here (almost a year ago, jeez!) he made sure Terry knew this was his home too. That he was going to have two homes from then on, and that he should feel comfortable and welcome in both. He explained that our place was smaller but that we would find nooks where he could play, that we would manage somehow and that without a doubt, we could be as happy as in the other house. Joseba really meant what he said, but none of us really believed it, and Terry, least of all. But he knows (because he is so smart as he shows me time after time) that he has little say in the actions and clumsy decisions adults take around him, that he is only eight and has to follow the rules of the game, changing homes without getting hurt while listening to his father and mother's arguments, treating the busybody witch respectfully (he never forgets to say thank you, please, or excuse me when he addresses me). But he sets some basic limits, and he has every right to, of course, and we should respect them. Like not hanging his drawing in our home. It's OK little one, if I were in your shoes I believe that I would behave the same way.

Limits and all, I think we are making progress and little by little adapting to each other. When have we had the opportunity to hang out, just the two of us, alone, for this long before? It seems to me that we are even conversing. This is our first time and Joseba won't be back until tomorrow; our relationship might improve. It might be because this boy is intelligent and I am not dumb. Although there are many ways to define intelligence, I prefer the following: intelligence is the ability to best adapt to different situations. Some might call it being practical. I am convinced that Terry is a practical person like his father. Yes, Joseba is a practical man, usually. Did Joseba act in a practical manner when he slept with me? Allowing his wife to catch us? It depends on how you look at it.

It is true that I will always wonder. If Victoria did not catch me in the bathroom, would we live in this house or would we still live under the secret lover label? Still dangling from Joseba's promise that he would leave his wife as the cliché states? I must live with that doubt but, since I am a practical person too, I will not dwell too much on what could have been. I only give importance to what is. That's the key.

And this is what I have. Here I have this pale child, with his two big ears, the one who has returned his drawing to the entry (so he doesn't forget it on Thursday when he leaves this house), the one who does not shut up, stricken with a chat-attack. He is sure excited about this Gunpowder Plot story.

". . . and this is why today they light bonfires in Mother's land, all over England. To remember Guy Fawkes's plot. My grandparents did it too when Mother was a child. They made a bonfire in the yard, on November fifth, at night. Mother loved it."

"Here's your yogurt." Every time someone mentions Victoria I get the urge to change subjects. I can't help it.

"They roasted potatoes in the fire and invited all Mother's friends to eat them and drink Coca-Cola." He does what I tell him and keeps talking between spoonfuls of yogurt. "And do you know what? They throw an effigy that represents Guy

Fawkes into the flames. That's how they reenact November the fifth."

"With bonfires? Throwing an effigy into the flames?"

"Yes, like on the Eve of Saint John's here, which by the way, is not for a while, eh?"

"Yes, a long while . . . sorry."

"And if we make a bonfire?" He said, ". . . we make," but who is he referring to? He and I? Joseba, he, and I? Or is he referring to Joseba, Victoria, and him?

"Yes, and we can jump over it, if you want." If Victoria could hear him . . .

"We were not allowed to make a bonfire in school, although all of us wanted to. We drew a bonfire and hung it on the wall and left Guy's doll next to it but it is not the same thing."

"Of course not. Why didn't you make the bonfire?"

"School rules," he said with resignation.

"You should request a real bonfire for next year. Otherwise, what do you have such a great yard for?"

I do not want to treat him as an adult but I don't want to act like a mother either. In part because I do not want to compete with Victoria anymore, and in part because I hope that I will have a better chance to win him over by playing the role of the understanding aunt.

"Would you prefer to live in England?"

I cannot deny that this is not an idle question. Actually, it is one of my fantasies that an enraged and betrayed Victoria returns home with her little son, ready to start a new life and definitively forgetting her cheating husband and his lover. This way Victoria's memories will dissipate from my mind. After many years, once the feelings calm down, we'll begin receiving colorful Christmas cards from Victoria and

Terry wishing us a happy new year, a sign that everything has returned to normalcy. Happy New Year!

I hate myself for having these thoughts, especially because of Joseba. It would be too hard for him to live away from his son. The situation in which we are now immersed is already quite hard for him, and the boy lives just a half hour from our place. But after all, nowadays it is so inexpensive and fast to go to England by flying on one of those new, low-cost airlines. No, I should stop fantasizing. Victoria will never leave. She has spent more years here than in her own country. Basically, though she will never admit it, she is one of us. She will always live a half hour from our house.

"It depends. Sometimes I would. For instance, today. If I were in Oxford now with my grandparents, we would make a bonfire in the garden, and eat hamburgers, as many as we wanted. And we'd drink Coca-Cola. And watch fireworks, but to live there forever . . . I don't know. I don't have any friends there. My friends live here."

"We can share a Coca-Cola if you want." I pray that there is at least one left in the refrigerator.

Terry reacts to my offer with unusual enthusiasm. I know that he is not supposed to drink caffeinated drinks but those are his parents' prohibitions. I am the cool aunt and I am going to play dumb. Thankfully, there are two Coca-Colas left. I grab one and pour it in two glasses. I hear the phone ring. Two possibilities: It could be Joseba calling from Madrid, to tell me about his job interview or it could be Victoria, calling to find out if the child is still alive. I answer the phone in the kitchen afraid of the second possibility, and my least favorite hunch is confirmed. She asks me if Terry could get on the phone.

A couple words about my relationship with Victoria.

There is no such thing. Our conversations are scripted and limited to two lines. For example, today's: "Good afternoon, this is Victoria. Is Terry home?" "Yes, here he is. Bye, Victoria." That is all.

In my opinion, this woman's behavior is quite odd. She has never uttered any insults, hateful words, or expressed any contempt toward me. She has acted with dignity since the day she entered the bathroom and found me using her hair dryer. Since she threw Joseba out, she has never tried to talk things out, clarify things, or fix the situation. As far as I know, she has not asked Joseba for any explanations. She has accepted reality and has limited herself to play the role of the humble, cheated woman. It is very suspicious. Sometimes I think that since revenge is a dish served cold, she must be hatching an evil plan that I'll need to suffer when I least expect it. The more time goes by, the crueler will be her revenge because it will catch me off guard. Moreover, I often think that Terry can be part of this postponed revenge. He is the mole, the one who infiltrates my life, the one who knows our house, the one who compiles precise information with his naïve look, waiting for the right time to reveal the plot.

I tell Terry that he can use the telephone in the living room because his mom wants to talk to him.

"Mommy!"

I stay in the kitchen, close the door to give him some privacy and stare at the magnets on the refrigerator. I think of not hanging up the phone at this end in an effort to find out what kind of a conspiracy against me the mother and son are plotting. But I don't dare, not because of feelings of guilt but because I am afraid that Terry may discover me. I just limit myself to gluing my ear to the kitchen door. Terry begins talking very fast. I can't understand anything he says.

Then he quiets down and only utters isolated words like; Yes? Really? Then he begins talking again and I think (it is just a thought) that he says my name, that he is talking about me. Finally he blows a loud kiss for his mother and hangs up. I remain in the kitchen staring at the magnets for one more minute trying to hide my curiosity. I finally leave the kitchen holding two glasses of Coca-Cola that have lost their fizz.

Terry is back on the sofa, looking at *King Lear*. I hand him the fullest glass of Coca-Cola.

"Thank you."

"You're welcome."

He finishes the drink in two gulps and burps to show his satisfaction.

"Excuse me," he says politely as usual.

"No worries. How's your mom?" I ask him mechanically.

"Good. At work. I think she feels guilty."

"Guilty?" I did not expect that answer.

"Yes, she told me a long time ago that we would make a bonfire in the backyard next to the barbeque to celebrate November the fifth, and that I could invite all my friends. But she had to leave for work. She is always gone. I don't know why she has to work that much if Father pays her child support every month."

His comment catches me off guard. Terry hardly speaks about his mom in front of me. He acts as if he has made a pact of silence with someone. But now, he is not only talking about his mother but about his feelings for her. Except the reference to the child support (a direct stabbing), his words completely catch me by surprise.

Am I, by chance, becoming softer? Is it compassion that I'm feeling? Poor abandoned child. Here he is, eating fruit with a stranger, a witch, on a holiday he should be celebrating. At least I gave him some Coca-Cola. I have that working in my favor even though by the time he drinks it, it's flat. He has traces of Coca-Cola around his lips. He is once again gazing at his colorful book. It looks as if he is turning the pages against his will. I must admit, his situation is not an easy one. I regret my cunning thoughts against him. After all, he's a child, a vulnerable child.

But I am not that easily fooled. It is a trait of intelligent people to be manipulative and to know how to take advantage of emotional blackmail. I am aware of it. I have my own tricks. I am alert.

"It's OK Terry, you'll celebrate it next year. Besides, in the mean time we have Saint John's Eve. We can make a bonfire then."

"Yes, but is not the same. It was supposed to be tonight . . ."

"Would you like another Coca-Cola?"

"No, because I won't be able to fall sleep."

I check the time discreetly. It's six twenty. It is already dark outside. I hate November.

"May we make a bonfire here?"

I make a face showing fear and I hope that, as smart as he is, he can read it so I don't need to say a word. But he answers me with the smile of an innocent child waiting for a response from me.

"You mean here, inside the house?" Are you crazy, wicked child?

"Well, inside or . . ."

"That's impossible, Terry."

"And on the balcony?"

"On the balcony?"

"It's easy. We can use newspapers and a big container to

control the perimeter of the fire. Should we do it? Let's do it."

"Perimeter of the fire . . ." what is he talking about? I shake my head but Terry continues smiling at me. He is tough. I must think a little before answering. I must study the choices. Yes, we could make a fire on the balcony. Of course that is one of our possibilities. He would be ecstatic. Our relationship would strengthen. But I know that making a fire on the balcony is stupid, no question. A stupid act that doesn't help in the reenactment of Guy Fawkes's Treason Plot. But sometimes you can make children happy without much because they can fill the gaps in reality with their magical, symbolic imagination, beyond all logic.

And, why not? I could ask myself. It looks like the boy knows a lot about setting a fire perimeter. It could be beautiful to see Terry's face lit by the fire. We could warm our hands on this cold November evening. We could throw everything we don't like in the fire (is this the objective of this holiday?) The balcony is not very big but if the fire is small enough . . .

Terry senses doubt in my face and jumps off the sofa; he seems to be looking for old newspapers. So, is it decided? Am I going to leave the control of the situation in hands of a small arsonist? But why do I call him an arsonist? An arsonist's objective is fire itself. He finds fire pleasurable. But I think Terry's objectives may be others. He wants to use fire as a tool. After all, he couldn't care less about fire or about the evil Guy Fawkes.

Yes, thankfully I have taken my time to think about this.

Just picture a fire on my balcony and the both of us around it. Anything could go wrong, for example, a spark can light the curtain on fire. We will hardly have any time to call the firefighters; they will rescue us using their long ladders (that's in the best of cases, if they get to us in time, of course); we'll need to explain what happened (I should say, I'll need to); no one will understand the Guy Fawkes story; they will see me as a fool; Victoria's exasperation will be colossal; the judge will stop Terry's visitations; Joseba will never forgive me.

It is quite possible.

Let's say that nothing goes wrong, that the flames do not spread out beyond the perimeter of the fire. Even in a controlled situation, a neighbor might see the flames from her window. We have many neighbors across the street that have nothing better to do than look out the window, out of boredom. One of those busybody neighbors, without giving it a second thought, will call the fire department; she'll want to be a hero, get on television and then the same chain of events will unfold, the ladder, the dubious explanations, Victoria's and the judge's decisions . . . all the way to Joseba not forgiving me. To the point at which I do not want to arrive, that is. I would not like this ending but, wouldn't this ending be to Terry's and Victoria's liking? I am pretty sure it would. And it is now when I realize what is all this about. Guy Fawkes's story, the telephone call at the right time, this fire fantasy.

I see it quite clearly.

"No, Terry. Sit down. We are not going to make a fire. You can do it next year in your house, with your mother."

Terry was looking for a magazine on the shelves in the living room when my sharp tone has taken him by surprise and has made him stop in his tracks. He looks at me incredulously. It looks like he wants to say something but he does not. He sighs. He is a good boy and must comply. He does not have another choice. He returns to the indent he's left in the sofa, downcast. He takes Shakespeare's booklet and throws it on the floor.

"Pick it up, Terry."

"I don't want to."

"I told you to pick it up."

"And I said I don't want to."

What do I care if that damn book is on the floor.

"Very well. Don't pick it up."

This is how you control this type of situation. I return to the armchair. From here I can see that Terry's eyes are full of tears.

"Terry, please, don't cry. Do you think that your mom would let you make a fire on the balcony?"

"If my mom were here, everything would be different."

"Yes, of course. But we won't act silly because of it, right? It can be dangerous."

At this point, he is sobbing and I wonder if I am mistaken. That perhaps there is no plot here. That the child is lonely and just wants to make a fire, that's all. That he misses his mother and his father too.

"C'mon Terry, tell me something about King Lear."

It seems to work. He is calming down. He stops crying. He has a runny nose.

"A Kleenex?"

"Here."

"You asked me earlier what happened to Guy Fawkes."

I say yes, even though I do not recall. I am surprised that he still wants to talk to me. His face is flushed. He won't be sick, will he? I would not know what to do if that were the case.

"They caught him and charged him with high treason. And since that crime was very serious, the most serious in those days, the punishment was awful."

"Well, you don't need to give me all the details."

"They took him to the town square," the crying hiccups

break his words, and it is too bad because he is trying to use a scary inflection while telling the story, which loses tension as result of his hiccups. "They hanged him right there but not to his death because before it, they sliced him open from head to toe. Just like that, with a single slash." Terry makes an explicit movement directed to an imaginary Guy Fawks and, *hip!* goes a hiccup. "They cut his testicles and threw them to the fire, before his own eyes. Then they stripped out his bowels one by one and threw them onto the fire too. His innards and that stuff. Everything. The very last organ they pulled out was his heart because they wanted to keep him alive for as long as they could. Finally, they cut off his head. And other body parts too. And they kept them out there so people would see what happened to those who conspired and they would not dare come up with any other plots.

"Is that what they did?"

"Yes, exactly."

"Who told you that story?" I can't believe it's true.

"Everyone knows it."

"Really?"

"It was very common in those days. They show it in the movies too."

"Common?"

"Yes, but . . . you know what? They only punished men that way. They would have mercy upon traitorous women and they just burn them directly without dismembering them."

He no longer has hiccups. He stands up. He hesitates. He would like to go to his room and slam the door. Period. Send a clear message. It would be a great ending for the scene. But it is funny, this is a small apartment and therefore, Terry does not have his own room, he can't go anywhere. He will need to stay in front of me, and me next to him, that's it. Gazing at each other, perhaps in silence, until tomorrow, or forever, in this living room.

Trapped.

With no escape.

We are not sure why.

Acknowledgments

Aurelia Arkotxa, "Cordelia," "Hitz-estalaktitak," "Kaki-ondoa," "Stabat mater," and "Beribilez." From *Fragmentuak* (Eibar, Gipuzkoa: Utriusque Vasconia, 2006).

Uxue Apaolaza Larrea, "Karrotxoa," and "Familian." From *Umeek gezurra esaten dutenetik* (Donostia-San Sebastián: Erein, 2005).

Maite Gonzalez Esnal, "Hegoak ebaki nahi zizkion" From *Gutiziak* (Tafalla, Navarre: Txalaparta, 2000).

Eider Rodriguez, "Hazia." From *Katu jendea* (Donostia-San Sebastián: Elkar, 2010).

Miren Agur Meabe, "Liliaren perlak edo nola aldatu zitzaizkion Doltzari izena eta izana," and "Doltzari ama agertu." From *Zazpi Orduak* (Donostia-San Sebastián: Elkar, 2010).

Ana Urkiza, "Urrutiko lokarriak," and "Mutila egiten, Errauskiñe berria." From *Bekatuak* (Donostia-San Sebastián: Elkar, 2005).

Arantxa Iturbe, "Baietz ile kizkurra izan," and "Bi grano." From *Lehenago zen berandu* (Irun, Gipuzkoa: Alberdania, 1997) and *Gutiziak* (Tafalla, Navarre: Txalaparta, 2000).

Jasone Osoro Igartua, "Maitasuna puzzle bat da." From

Korapiloak (Donostia-San Sebastián: Elkar 2001).

Garazi Kamio Anduaga, "Panenka." From *Beste norbaiten zapatak* (Donostia-San Sebastián: Elkar, 2012).

Ixiar Rozas, "Korronteak." From Mende berrirako ipuinak. *Antologia* (Donostia-San Sebastián: Erein, 2005). Published as "A Draft." From An Anthology of Basque Short Stories (Reno: Center for Basque Studies, 2004)

Arantxa Urretabizkaia Bejarano, "Espero zaitudalako." From *Aspaldian espero zaitudalako ez nago sekula bakarrik* (Donostia-San Sebastián: Erein, 1983).

Begoña Bilbao Alboniga, "Isuritako ura ez da batzen." From *Ipuin izugarriak* (Donostia-San Sebastián: Elkar 2004).

Irati Elorrieta, "Paisaia urratuak." From *Orgasmus* (Tafalla, Navarre: Txalaparta, 2010).

Uxue Alberdi Estibaritz, "Gifts." From *Euli giro* (Zarautz, Gipuzkoa: Susa, 2013).

Karmele Jaio Eiguren, "Ultrasounds." From *Ez naiz ni* (Donostia-San Sebastián, Elkar, 2012).

Irati Jimenez Uriarte, *Laranja azalaren negarra* (Donostia-San Sebastián: Kutxa Fundazioa, 2008).

Katixa Agirre Miguélez, "Guy Fawksen traizioa." From *Habitat* (Donostia-San Sebastián: Elkar 2009).

About the Translator

Nere Lete earned her MFA in translation from the University of Iowa and is currently an associate professor of Basque and director of the Basque Studies Minor at Boise State University. She has translated many Basque writers including Bernardo Atxaga, Eider Rodriguez, Jokin Muñoz, Jose Antonio Loidi, and Xabier Lete. Her translations have been published by the Center for Basque Studies (UNR), *Hayden's Ferry Review* (Arizona State University) and *Inventory* (Princeton University). She has also worked as a voice-over actress and script adaptor for Basque television. She translated all of the stories for this book except for the previously published story "A Draft."

Linda White and Elizabeth Macklin additionally translated the story "A Draft" by Ixiar Rozas, which was originally published in *An Anthology of Basque Short Stories*, published by the Center for Basque Studies in 2004.